With a population small enough to fit comfortably into the bottom third of a New York skyscraper, Hope, Arkansas, is a city in name only. It still managed to become the birthplace of a US president, Bill Clinton.

The Language of Cities

Deyan Sudjic

PENGUIN BOOKS

PENGUIN BOOKS

UK | USA | Canada | Ireland | Australia
India | New Zealand | South Africa

Penguin Books is part of the Penguin Random House group of companies whose addresses can be found at global.penguinrandomhouse.com.

First published by Allen Lane 2016
Published in Penguin Books 2017

004

Set in 8.7/11.745 pt Sabon LT Std
Typeset by Jouve (UK) Milton Keynes
Printed in Great Britain by Clays Ltd, St Ives plc

A CIP catalogue record for this book is available from the British Library

ISBN: 978-0-141-98059-1

www.greenpenguin.co.uk

Penguin Random House is committed to a sustainable future for our business, our readers and our planet. This book is made from Forest Stewardship Council® certified paper.

Contents

Chapter One

What is a City

'City' is a word used to describe almost anything. A tiny settlement in the mid-West, with fewer than 10,000 people, and nothing more than a sheriff to represent civic authority, is called a city. So is Tokyo, with a population approaching 40 million, an urban structure based on multiple electoral districts, a parliamentary chamber, a governor, a prefectural government employing 250,000 people and a multi-billion dollar budget.

If anywhere can be defined as a city, then the definition runs the risk of meaning nothing. A city is made by its people, within the bounds of the possibilities that it can offer them: it has a distinctive identity that makes it much more than an agglomeration of buildings. Climate, topography and architecture are part of what creates that distinctiveness, as are its origins. Cities based on trade have qualities different from those that were called into being by manufacturing. Some cities are built by autocrats, others have been shaped by religion. Some cities have their origins in military strategy or statecraft.

These are not generic elements that always produce the same outcomes. Many cities have a river; but the Seine is unique and an essential part of what makes Paris different from Berlin and the Spree. Hong Kong is a trading city, so are Dubai and Hamburg, but they are unmistakably themselves. Not all the characteristics of distinctiveness are positive. The ruined hulk of a beaux arts theatre that is now used as a car park is a very specific part of the identity of only one city, Detroit.

In material terms, a city can be defined by how close together its people gather to live and work, by its system of government, by its transport infrastructure and by the functioning of its sewers. And, not least, by its economic potential. One definition of a city is that it is a wealth-creating machine that can, at the minimum, make the poor not quite as poor as they were. A real city offers its citizens the freedom to be what they want to be. The idea of what makes a city is more elusive, but is as significant as the data. Just a short walk from the scars left in the fabric of New York by the destruction of the Twin Towers, the words of two American poets have been spelled out in heavy block capitals cast, letter by letter, in bronze into a sequence of railings next to the Hudson. They lack precision, and fail to offer prescriptions for urbanism, yet they have resonances missing in more materialistic definitions of a city.

Walt Whitman's tone is that of a soaring eulogy:

> City of the sea! . . .
> City of wharves and stores! city of tall façades of marble and iron!
> Proud and passionate city! mettlesome, mad, extravagant city!

Whitman's first two lines, which would mean little to the 45th president of the United States, are missing. They reflect an even more important measure of urbanity:

> City of the world! (for all races are here;
> All the lands of the earth make contributions here)

And then, a little further along the waterfront, with the litter of new high-rises lining the New Jersey shore visible across the river, Frank O'Hara is more laconic:

> One need never leave the confines of New York to get all the greenery one wishes – I can't even enjoy a blade of grass unless I know there's a subway handy, or a record store or some other sign that people do not totally regret life.

The verses are the product of an unusually enlightened piece of place-making under the lugubrious shadow of what used to be called the World Financial Center, which paid for it. The Iranian-born artist Siah Armajani selected the verses and designed their physical setting to create somewhere for office workers to feel the sun, and smell the tang of the Hudson in the air.

Whether the World Financial Center itself, formed of six distinct buildings totalling eight million square feet, lives up to Whitman's idea of a city is an open question. The development summed up the essence of a certain approach to city-making, at a particular moment in the evolution of New York. That this approach, replicated all around the world, is no longer current is demonstrated in the renaming of the site. The World Financial Center survived 9/11, but is called Brookfield Place now. Deloitte, Fidelity and the *Wall Street Journal* are based at 200 Liberty Street, a tower which, in the way favoured by developers when it was built in the 1980s, used to be called One World Financial Center, just as Merrill Lynch is at 250 Vesey Street, once known as Four World Financial Center.

The new addresses are a gesture towards Jane Jacobs, the greatest critic of big-picture planning. They reflect a belated realization that monster-size blocks disrupt street patterns. But simply giving a million square feet of office space in a 40-floor tower a street address is not going to turn it into a piece of an intimate, pedestrian-scaled city. Brookfield Place is still an urban monoculture, created on landfill. It offers a civilized enough place in which to eat a sandwich lunch, it has an ice rink and an events programme to encourage shoppers at weekends. At Christmas the Winter Garden is lit up every night.

Brookfield Place is owned by the same development company that controls Canary Wharf in London, which has a no less ambitious public art programme, and a similar abundance of places to eat. Like Brookfield Place, Canary Wharf accommodates the local outposts of global companies from American Express to Nomura. They cluster together, in all but interchangeable surroundings, like the present-day version of the kontor compounds – the word means 'counting house' or 'office' – established by the Hanseatic

League in the fifteenth century. Hansa traders spread out across northern Europe, from the free cities of the Baltic, setting up enclaves as far away as the Steelyard in London. They kept themselves to themselves and took their architecture with them everywhere they went, much in the manner of twenty-first-century investment bankers using their American decorators to construct cinemas, swimming pools and wine cellars beneath their terraced houses in Holland Park.

Walt Whitman spent his later life in Camden, New Jersey, which suggests that while he appreciated the qualities of a great metropolitan city, he himself did not feel the need to spend his time in one. Frank O'Hara, on the other hand, lived a life on East 9th Street that could only have been possible in what we understand to be a city in the modern sense. It was the life of a gay man in the New York of the 1950s, a city which demonstrated the limits of its liberalism by becoming the first jurisdiction in the United States not to legalize homosexuality, but to define it as a misdemeanour rather than a felony.

O'Hara's life could be seen as the product of two mutually interdependent qualities: urbanity and modernity. In the modern world one important definition of a city might be that it allows homosexuals to live as they choose, just as it offers tolerance for the religious and, as Whitman suggests, welcomes its citizens from all nations and all races. But tolerance is not without responsibilities on the part of both host and newcomer, as the current fear that the migrants now fleeing war in Syria, Iraq and Afghanistan are bringing misogyny with them demonstrates.

There is comforting evidence that those cities that have exhibited tolerance have flourished ahead of those that have not. Amsterdam became the centre of the world's most powerful trading state in the seventeenth century in part because it encouraged the persecuted – Huguenots, Jews, Puritans and others – to live there. In turn, it was the model for the city that Peter the Great set out to build as Russia's window to the world, though he was more successful at replicating Amsterdam's architectural qualities than embracing the same tolerance in St Petersburg.

But the idea of an open city, celebrated by Whitman and O'Hara, is not the only basis for cities and their growth, even the ones that the modern world admires. Athens was built by slave owners, and there was no popular democracy in Rome or Renaissance Florence. Moscow, Beijing and Tokyo still demonstrate the pattern left by the autocracies that built them. The Kremlin, the Forbidden City and the Imperial Palace are the monuments of an urban system that was built around a single all-powerful individual. Each of them had a palace at the centre, surrounded by an inner city of retainers and kin, and an outer zone for merchants and labourers excluded from the court. These were systems developed to impose control over the masses. From the earliest classical cities, elites have feared the power of the mob and have done all that they could to suppress it. The rise of the industrial city, from the end of the eighteenth century in Europe, brought these fears to feverish levels. Observers of the huge growth of modern cities began to use metaphors of sickness and disease to describe them. By 1830 William Cobbett was calling London the 'Great Wen', a tumour on the face of rural England.

Absolute numbers have preoccupied some demographers since at least 1798, when Thomas Malthus concluded, so far mistakenly, that populations rise much faster than we can increase the rate at which we grow the food needed to feed ourselves. The fear of the uncontrollable growth of cities and the disorder that came with it was as threatening as the prospect of mass starvation. The realization that cities now account for the majority of the planet's population is more recent and has triggered a fresh set of anxieties.

To the privileged few living in the affluent enclaves of Mumbai, with its hundreds of thousands of pavement dwellers, or in Nairobi with Kibera, its huge slum clinging to a railway track, and in so many other similarly polarized cities, those enclaves seem more like islands of order, under siege from the dispossessed pressing in from all sides, rather than communities.

In 1950, cities were predominantly creations of the rich world, which accounted for 60 per cent of the urban population even if it included the relatively poor in addition to the well off. Now that 70 per cent of city dwellers come from the developing world, cities are more likely to be poor in absolute terms. Since the turn of the twenty-first century, Lagos and Dhaka have each attracted 1,000 new people every day of every year. They come not from other cities but partly from natural population increase: from rural Bangladesh for Dhaka; and, in the case of Lagos, from throughout sub-Saharan Africa and beyond. For a while this transition to majority urban was presented, perhaps overexcitedly, as an event with the same kind of potential significance in the evolution of mankind as the transformation of our nomadic hunter-gatherer ancestors into settled farmers, or even the discovery of life on Mars. But when it actually took place it did not appear as dramatic in its immediate impact as had been advertised.

When the UN started talking about the shift to the cities at the start of this century, it left unexplored the question of definitions. If half the world's people were not yet living in cities before 2005, exactly what had they been living in? Was it the 'country' (a term with no clear meaning)? Was it in those towns that were somehow not cities? Were they in the suburbs of towns and cities, or were they living in something else altogether?

In fact there are as just as many kinds of 'not cities' as there are varieties of cities. Life on a farm, a smallholding, a country estate, or in a fishing village, is not life in a city. A mining town extracting copper in the high Chilean desert does not offer city life either. Life on a military base, in one of the former Soviet Union's closed penal colonies, in a Bangladeshi community whose members risk

Autocratic societies build capitals to enforce their hierarchical nature. Typically the political and religious court is at the centre with a merchant city huddled at the castle gates, and proletarian suburbs spreading to the horizon. Moscow, Beijing and Tokyo are all crowded cities, with empty acres of privilege at their heart fringed by skyscrapers. The Kremlin (above), begun in 1147 as a wooden stockade, is still a centre of power.

Chapter One

The Japanese emperor moved from Kyoto to Tokyo in 1868. Since then, the palace has not changed, while the world's largest city has grown up around its moats.

The Ming dynasty made Beijing its capital in 1420. Mao spent his first night as the supreme leader of the People's Republic of China in its palace.

their health breaking up ships for scrap, in a squatter settlement on the edge of Brazzaville, in a refugee camp on the Turkish border with Syria, is in every case far removed from life in what we understand a city to be. They lack the material resources of a city, and they are missing the qualities that Whitman and O'Hara celebrated.

Urbanization has brought massive change but, to paraphrase William Gibson, the creator of cyberpunk fiction, it is not uniformly distributed. Rural and urban life is not always sharply differentiated. In some African cities, the rural poor move to the outskirts of cities that offer little more in the way of urbanity than the settlements they left behind. These are cities that skipped industrialization. Many of their citizens support themselves through market gardening. This might still turn out to be as much of an advantage as a handicap. A city that can feed itself could one day find itself with important advantages compared with one that can't. Kenya, with an absence of copper-wire fixed phone lines, was able to leapfrog old technologies and pioneer mobile banking. The architect Norman Foster is exploring an equivalent jump in transport terms, with a project to devise a drone airport in Rwanda to facilitate deliveries to remote settlements with unreliable roads.

Elsewhere, the shift from the country to the city is more clear-cut. In China, millions of peasants moved, most likely illegally, to work on construction sites in Shanghai or on iPhone assembly lines in Shenzhen. They left poor farms and, because China does not allow its people free internal movement, they found themselves living in hostels among clumps of high-rises or in shacks on construction sites, with very restricted civic rights. In India, a nation whose constitution guarantees freedom of movement, Untouchables are still moving from rural oppression to the slums of Mumbai to find work and escape caste persecution.

A closer understanding of these 'not cities' and a comparison with some of the emerging cities, and of older ones too, shows that the borderline between them is porous. The essential qualities of what might be called 'urbanity', or 'citiness' as the sociologist Saskia Sassen once described it, can ebb and flow.

Installing generously appointed, well-maintained latrines with showers and laundry rooms in a Mumbai slum such as Dharavi is a step towards a more dignified kind of urban life. Building a school in a refugee camp, and installing electric street lights around it, goes further. Mark Zuckerberg's plans to beam the potential for high-speed broadband connections by satellite into remote zones of Africa injects another kind of 'citiness' into places where it does not yet exist. All these actions can make 'not cities' into something a bit more city-like. And, conversely, there are ways in which cities can start to lose the qualities that make them urban, rather than merely random collections of buildings.

It is not difficult to pick out the things which signal that a city is in trouble, or in decline. Multiple varieties of deprivation for its poor, high rates of infant mortality, rampant violent crime, multinational companies shedding jobs as they leave, broken-down public transport, an airport losing direct flights and civic budgets that do not balance. Cities in terminal trouble can no longer protect their citizens from violence, enforce the law in the face of corruption, or even offer them clean water and reliable supplies of electricity.

Measures of success are less clear. Growing population numbers can have variable meanings. Smaller cities want to attract more people but, after a certain point, increasing numbers can threaten to overwhelm cities. To succeed, a city needs to offer its citizens security, safety and freedom of choice.

After *The Death and Life of Great American Cities*, Jane Jacobs wrote a less well-known book, *The Economy of Cities*, which convincingly suggests that the most successful cities are those that have more than one kind of success and are continually able to reinvent themselves. So Los Angeles has been able to move

Chapter One

Oxford, the English-speaking world's oldest university (top), has roots in the Christian monasteries of the early middle ages. Isfahan (bottom), like Oxford, was once a capital, and grew around religious institutions and the educational system that supported them.

on from an economy once based on fruit to high-tech aerospace, from movies and music to banking, as the economic basis for its existence. But Detroit went straight from building nine in every 10 of the world's motor cars to a population implosion and bankruptcy.

In some but not all countries, this recent wave of urbanization has increased the national dominance of those cities that are growing at the fastest rate. At least one Briton in every eight is a Londoner, and a majority of births in London in 2014 were to parents not themselves born there. One Turk in every six lives in Istanbul. It is different in India. Mumbai, with 22 million people, the country's second-largest city just behind New Delhi, has getting on for twice as many residents as Istanbul but it accounts for less than one in every 60 Indians. The country's political class has lingering memories of the Gandhian ideology on which independence was founded, and so has a vestigial antipathy towards the very idea of the city. India was to be rooted in the self-sufficiency of village life. It was an antipathy which easily merged with the horror of the Anglo-Saxons at the industrial city that they had invented. The attitudes that India's Oxbridge-educated elite picked up, in some cases at first hand from John Ruskin and William Morris, encouraged them to see cities as alien creations that reduced their people to servile squalor.

Population numbers for cities, even when they are based on reliable census data, can never be entirely accurate. Despite their apparent mathematical precision, they are based on a narrow idea of what constitutes a city, one defined by political boundaries. These boundaries do not necessarily delineate actual cities any more than the colonial maps of Africa reflected ethnic or national identity. But city boundaries can become self-fulfilling prophecies. For better or worse, they define the ways that various levels of government interact to make a city work. To define a real city, rather than an administrative expression, involves a more imaginative process.

Chapter One

What is called Mexico City is not one single political entity. A population of some 20 million people is spread across 1,400 square kilometres, over three or more jurisdictions: the Federal District; the State of Mexico; and a cluster of other municipalities caught up in a city that grows in bursts. Sometimes this growth is through the precision-planned creation of illegal settlements. Hundreds, if not thousands, of squatters descend in organized groups to take command of the land in raids that are beyond the power of conventional planning authorities to prevent. In a few quick moves, they create makeshift homes, tapping into electricity and water lines. Elsewhere much growth is through legal commercial development that is undermining the qualities of urban life in Mexico City by its focus on nothing more than the provision of minimal housing.

Mexico City was once spoken of as if it were doomed to be the biggest settlement on the planet. It was probably the first of the twentieth century's new megacities to make an impression on the wider world, portrayed as an unstoppable eruption of humanity swamping the landscape to reach the horizon in every direction. The predictions in the 1970s were that Mexico City was well on the way to becoming a megalopolis of 30 million people or more. As it turned out, that has not happened. The population of the wider city centre is static, and some of its denser historic areas have been in decline. What growth there is now concentrates in the urban sprawl beyond city limits in the administrative control of the State of Mexico. The middle class is moving out into areas where gated communities are not just for the privileged.

Mexico City grew fast from the 1940s when it began to lose its former incarnation as the Garden of Eden, blessed with a near-perfect climate, reminiscent of the golden age of Los Angeles, but physically shaped by the remains of its Aztec and Spanish past as represented by flower-studded baroque courtyards and by the presence of the surrounding mountains and the famous lake. The photochemical smog that accompanied the city's discovery of the motor car, through the medium of the locally produced Volkswagens that once monopolized its streets, made its growth look particularly threatening. That toxic haze was not helped by Mexico City's extreme altitude and its mountains, two elements that conspire to entrap the city's pollution in the brown cloud that seems to thicken under the wings of descending aircraft. The more it grew, the more the by-products of that growth seemed to have life-threatening consequences for its inhabitants.

Certainly Mexico is huge: 20 million or so people may now live in the city itself, in the Federal District, and in the urbanized sprawl around it. But that is a close match for Shanghai, New York and London – when their respective city regions are taken into account. All three of them have their own disparities in wealth, even if Mexico City's seem more violent, more entrenched, and Mexico has not had 50 years of Mao and Marx to damp down the sometimes chaotic lawlessness of the country in the way in which China has.

There are street children and kidnappings and water shortages in Mexico City, and a sewage system at the limits of its original design life. But Mexico City never became the horror story that it sometimes threatened. Its growth has started to taper off, almost to the point where one could begin to consider the idea that growth might be self-limiting. Its reputation most likely has something to do with its proximity to the United States. For those with a taste for disaster tourism, Mexico City is more convenient to get to than other huge urban sprawls such as Lagos or Tehran.

Mexico City has had more than the explosive growth of the flight of the dispossessed from the countryside to contend with. Its overlapping political boundaries have resulted in different power bases pursuing different, sometimes mutually contradictory, strategies that failed to come to a shared view of what the place needs in order to function properly. Mexico City has within it the elements of a global city, both negative and positive. It has slick business parks and boutique hotels, and it is losing industrial jobs to China and to the NAFTA factories on the US border. It is displaying the chronic symptoms of uneven development in its lurch towards the global economy. It's a city in which illegal land sales blight development in some areas, and the informal economy extends much further than the all-pervasive street traders and its 120,000 taxis.

Its metro system was its pride and joy when Mexico hosted the Olympics in 1968, an event that was intended to mark the high point of the country's attempts to present itself as a modern state. The metro was the best that Mexico could afford when it was built but has failed to adapt to what has been going on around it; and parts of the city have outgrown it.

Mexico City's recent mayors reflect the city's diverse qualities. The city as governed by Andrés Manuel López Obrador was a heterogeneous, lumpy mix of the nineteenth and twenty-first centuries. He was the third elected mayor after the Institutional Revolutionary Party relaxed its long grip on the country. He later became the presidential candidate of the Party of the Democratic Revolution.

The distinctive flavour of Obrador's term in office included funding a free circus installed in the Zócalo, the city's main square, complete with exotic wild animals; and the remarks that he is reported to have made when a mob beat a thief to death in a suburb just beyond the city: this was, he asserted 'the real Mexico speaking, and village traditions of justice should be respected'. Obrador's opponent in the presidential election that followed used a clip from that speech in a television attack ad that was later banned. Mexico is clearly also a part of the modern world, and a different aspect of Obrador's populist measures was to cancel City Hall's Microsoft software licences, and to adopt Linux free operating systems instead. His two most visible legacies to the city reflected the paradoxes of his policies. On the one hand, he introduced dedicated bus lanes, modelled on the precedents of Bogotá in Colombia and Curitiba in Brazil, that have transformed public transport in the city. On the other, his personal *grand projet*, the massive and quixotic plan to create a double-decker urban highway, the Distribuidor Vial, asked more questions than it answered. It was enormously expensive, and appeared to benefit only the relatively wealthy car-owning residents of the privileged areas through which it passes, in a city in which commutes of three hours are forced on the maids who work for the rich but live in far-distant *barrios*.

It is arguable that a city which lacks a democratic government cannot be understood as a city at all. Dubai, where less than 15 per cent of its residents are citizens, is a fundamental challenge to the idea of what a city can be. On census day in 2013 it counted 2.1 million permanent residents with another 900,000 people temporarily present, including tourists and commuters based in neighbouring emirates coming in to work and then returning to their own jurisdictions.

The census also revealed a massive gender imbalance, with just one woman to every three men. In itself this is a reflection of the two versions of Dubai. One is a city of high-rises, hotels and indoor ski slopes, the other is a vast labour camp that warehouses hundreds of thousands of men, mainly from the Islamic communities of Asia, who build and service the neighbouring city and have no right to remain once their contracts expire. Yet in its regional context, Dubai is certainly a cosmopolitan city, one which is prepared to countenance a level of cultural and social freedom that many of its neighbours will not.

Many cities lack full control of their political destinies. New

York's mayor, for example, has little more than locally levied property taxes to count on. Much of the rest of the budget depends on coming to an accommodation with the Governor of New York State based in the imperial architecture of the science-fiction village that Nelson Rockefeller created in Albany. It is a division of powers that has left successive mayors struggling to deal with big employers who threaten to leave the city unless they are offered financial incentives to remain, incentives the young Donald Trump eagerly accepted.

There was no democratically accountable administration for London as a whole for the 15 years between Margaret Thatcher's abolition of the Greater London Council and Tony Blair's establishment of the Greater London Authority with a directly elected mayor. It was a void that pushed London to grow in often chaotic ways.

A city does not need to be a contiguous built form. What look like rural communities in upstate New York or in the Cotswolds are fully parts of the cities of which they are satellites. A former commissioner of the Metropolitan Police, Sir Ian Blair, once suggested that the borders of London could be understood, for the purposes of his operations, as stretching as far as Jamaica and Baghdad.

In 1851, London had more than two million people. It was by far the largest city in the world, twice the size of its nearest rival, Paris. That version of London would seem like a modest city now. By the official definition, London has 8.6 million people, but in practical terms it is a city of 18 million, straggling all the way from Ipswich to Bournemouth in an unforgiving tide of business parks and designer outlets, gated housing and logistics depots. There might be fields between them, but they are linked in a single economy. Those villages in Suffolk that are close enough to a railway station to deliver commuters to Liverpool Street in under 90 minutes are effectively as much a part of London as Croydon or Ealing, and they have house prices to prove it.

Is there a minimum size for a settlement to function as what we now think of as a city? And what is the impact on the life of an individual who is either unable, or unwilling, to live in such a place? In the eighteenth century, Adam Smith spent 10 years of his life in the Fife town of Kirkcaldy writing *The Wealth of Nations*, his treatise on economics that could be said to have changed the world. It is doubtful that his present-day equivalent could stay in Fife and do the same, even though its population is 50,000 now, more than 10 times what it was in his lifetime. Although he or she could consult every recent PhD in the world from a laptop on her kitchen table and travel to Edinburgh to look at the shelves in the university library, the only further-education institution in Smith's home is Fife College with its courses in Hair Care and Life Skills.

In the same way, cities demand a certain scale today if they are to have a major cultural impact. The Bauhaus was based first in Weimar and then Dessau, a town of 80,000 people in provincial Germany, and yet its ideas transformed the way that the world sees architecture and design. Its successor institutions, that now occupy the restored Bauhaus building, have little prospect of doing the same.

In the twenty-first century, power, influence and resources cluster in fewer and fewer places. Private equity firms are based in London or New York, even though there are always claims that this duopoly is about to be overturned by a new challenger. Once it was Frankfurt, then Hong Kong, now it is Singapore or Dubai that is talked about as a contender. There is as yet little sign of it actually happening. Film-makers base themselves in Los Angeles, Mumbai or Hong Kong and for the most part they stay there, despite the efforts of cities around the world to bribe them to move. It was not always this way: Berlin, London, Rome and Madrid, even Belgrade, all had active film-making studios once. Would-be fashion designers want to study in London, and show their work in Paris, Milan or New York, rather than in Moscow.

Digital entrepreneurs are in Silicon Valley and Bangalore. In so many of these fields, the same cities come up again and again. Their size is one of the key factors that distinguishes them in attracting investment and people ahead of their competitors. One million has become the generally assumed minimum size for a city to be able to support the attributes needed to measure up as a global centre, with an international airport, a university, creative industries, law courts and the rest.

Rome was the first city in history with a population of more than one million. It took another 1,800 years for London to eclipse its size and become a city of two million. At the start of the twentieth century, there were only 16 cities with more than one million people. Now there are more than 400, but it's unlikely that all but a few of them have the clout of their predecessors.

By a strict interpretation of that number such once-significant centres of urban civilization as Edinburgh, the city in which David Hume and Adam Ferguson set out to usher in the Age of Enlightenment in the company of 50,000 fellow citizens, or San Francisco, with fewer than 900,000 people today, would be ruled out.

As suggested earlier, it is questionable whether political boundaries are a true measure of a city's population. Within city limits, San Francisco is less than one million, but the Bay Area as a whole is more like seven million, and it is this that makes it possible for it to have the airport hub and the critical mass that it needs to function as a metropolis.

Cupertino, some 50 miles beyond San Francisco's city limits, has been calling itself a city since 1955. It houses Apple, one of the most powerful corporations on Earth which, in the last two decades, has utterly transformed the way that we consume and communicate. Cupertino has a population of 60,000. Is it, then, a city like Siena in the Middle Ages when it helped to create the modern banking system? Should it be regarded as less a city than the contemporary version of a remote monastery populated by devout adepts exploring all the possible names of God? More likely, we should see Cupertino as a suburb of San Francisco.

At the most fundamental level how should we understand the nature of the city? Are today's cities to be regarded as man-made artefacts of almost infinite complexity, like a smartphone that can perform remarkably well but nevertheless has its bugs and is prone to crashing yet which can be redesigned and improved? Or is a city to be regarded as more like a natural phenomenon? We can predict the weather but we can't yet make it rain.

Christopher Alexander, one-time architectural adviser to the Prince of Wales, provocatively titled his essay on the nature of urbanism 'A City is Not a Tree'. It's a paradoxical title. Alexander tried to make a distinction between what he claimed were cities that have arisen more or less spontaneously over many, many years, and those that have been deliberately created by designers and planners. Even though all cities are self-evidently the result of the deliberate act of human intervention (and, as such, are man-made rather than somehow natural, self-ordering systems), 'spontaneous' cities, according to Alexander, include Siena and Liverpool – for their supposed pragmatic, informal patterns of growth – and, more questionably, Kyoto and Manhattan, which are both planned on grids. He calls them 'natural' cities, in contrast to such 'artificial' cities as Levittown, Chandigarh and such British New Towns as Basildon and Cumbernauld. 'It is more and more widely recognized today that there is some essential ingredient missing from artificial cities. When compared with ancient cities that have acquired the patina of life, our modern attempts to create cities artificially are, from a human point of view, entirely unsuccessful.' For Alexander, an artificial city is a 'tree', its organization is too simple to allow the complex interactions of a richer, subtler organization.

> The tree of my title is not a green tree with leaves. It is the name of an abstract structure. I shall contrast it with

> another, more complex abstract structure called a semi-lattice. In order to relate these abstract structures to the nature of the city, I must first make a simple distinction.
>
> . . .
>
> Both the tree and the semilattice are ways of thinking about how a large collection of many small systems goes to make up a large and complex system. More generally, they are both names for structures of sets.
>
> . . .
>
> In a traditional society, if we ask a man to name his best friends and then ask each of these in turn to name their best friends, they will all name each other so that they form a closed group. A village is made up of a number of separate closed groups of this kind.
>
> But today's social structure is utterly different. If we ask a man to name his friends and then ask them in turn to name their friends, they will all name different people, very likely unknown to the first person; these people would again name others, and so on outwards. There are virtually no closed groups of people in modern society. The reality of today's social structure is thick with overlap – the systems of friends and acquaintances form a semilattice, not a tree.

Alexander went on to develop a number of semi-mystical ideas about cities and planning, notably in his book *A Pattern Language*, which has enjoyed cult status with Silicon Valley coders who see parallels in his ideas with their own obsessions. He had emerged from academic research at Yale, where he was an assistant to Serge Chermayeff working alongside the architect Norman Foster, although he clearly took somewhat different lessons from the experience in his violent rejection of modernism.

Alexander was one of many trying to fill the void in ideas for what to do about the city, which, as the race riots of the 1960s in the US and the middle-class flight to the suburbs throughout Europe and North America demonstrated, was in trouble.

Much of the developed world was losing its faith in planning and turning against the idea that professionals knew best. The high-rise utopias of modernist planning had failed to live up to the promises made for them. When even an internationally conspicuous housing project designed by a celebrated architect, such as the Pruitt–Igoe flats in St Louis, could be dynamited a decade after it was built, it was clear how much had gone wrong.

Alexander offered an alternative philosophical model to the conventional diagrams of planning systems. Peter Hall, the British urban scholar, and adviser to successive governments, took a more practical approach, even though he also set out to overturn conventional thinking on how to manage cities. Hall's book *Great Planning Disasters* took a scalpel to five fiascos, all of them intended to have been exercises in transformative planning. He looked at the absurdly expensive and inconclusive story of London's strategy to find a third airport, a story that, more than 40 years later, is still no nearer resolution. The book summed up a view of the dangers implicit in adopting big ideas about planning. They are expensive, they take too long and often they don't work.

If the professionals saw things this way, it was no wonder that in the wider world of activists, intellectuals and politicians, as well as the everyday victims of slum clearances and motorway construction, there was revulsion against any further evisceration of Europe's and North America's great cities. It was almost too late. For 30 years Robert Moses, New York's all-powerful master planner, had been building roads and demolishing neighbourhoods. From her vantage point in Greenwich Village, Jane Jacobs finally put a stop to his plans, and published her devastating attack on those who attempted drastic surgery on the fabric of the city. Small, she believed, was the future. Cities should be nurtured, not traumatized.

If, for Alexander, a city was not a tree, for Jacobs, a city was not a work of art. Which is to say that a city is never complete, and that it cannot be the product of a single vision. Together with Robert Caro, who wrote *The Power Broker*, a closely argued case for the prosecution against Robert Moses, Jacobs made the very idea of clean-slate urban transformation suspect. An economic crisis in the 1970s, troubling crime rates and New York's traumatic flirtation with bankruptcy triggered a flight for the suburbs. A combination of activism, professional uncertainty and weak finances created a reluctance to develop overarching approaches to cities that remained more or less unchallenged for two decades. Ideological conservatives presented laissez-faire non-planning as a more intelligent solution than heavy-handed state intervention. Houston, a city that supposedly has no restrictions on what land can be used for, and where anything is possible, was their model. In reality, a tightly written set of legal covenants do the job of zoning. For years, the professional planners devoted themselves to stopping things from happening, rather than achieving positive results. Attempts at positive intervention, it was assumed, would make things worse rather than better. But the idea of big-picture, gestural planning led by political will has refused to die. François Mitterrand set about an imperial makeover of Paris with his new museums, national library and ministries at the end of the 1980s. A little later his programme was followed by the transformation of Barcelona, a city in which architects, planners and politicians had suffered in the same prison cells during the years of Franco's dictatorship, and were close enough to each other to be able to embark jointly on the renewal of their city once the dictator had gone. It is true that there were protests about the gentrification of the red-light district into a tourist zone, and the destruction of the working-class Poblenou community on the waterfront. But the massive investment in infrastructure really did transform Barcelona. It was a city that went from crumbling neglect to becoming an architectural showcase that brought jobs, tourists and creative energy with it.

And as a result it became a model for other attempts to transform cities. It was a more worthwhile lesson than the seductively simple idea that a single building, in the Bilbao Guggenheim style, can transform a city all on its own. The reality in the Basque capital involved a decade of careful planning, investment in a new mass transit system, a new airport, education, hotels and the support of the European Regional Development Fund.

Sometimes it seems as if all the complex arguments about how we should understand the future of cities might boil down to the resolution of just two questions that represent polar opposites. Are we best served by dense cities or by sprawling suburbs? Is the market a better guide for shaping development than the state? They are the restricted range of options that keep appearing and reappearing around the world.

But perhaps there is another, even more fundamental, question to face up to. What can we really do in order to address what might be described as the urban bigger picture, in order to transform it to achieve positive effects? Are urban transformations actually possible? Or should we avoid the fallout from taking risks, and confine ourselves instead to taking small, incremental steps, and attempt to deal with our difficulties one pothole and one traffic jam at a time?

Critics of big-picture planning characterize it as being concerned more with the image of development than with its substance. It is presented as the product of egotistical politicians and their officials, sometimes incompetent or corrupt and always tending towards hubris. Instead those critics argue for a bottom-up approach.

The Paris of Haussmann and Napoleon III is still a model for those who take the opposite view and see the city as indeed being a work of art; a city that is capable of being completed and, as a result, ready to accept life in an urban steady state. This is not an entirely positive model. The Paris that is defined by the limits of the Périphérique is incapable of the kind of change that allows cities to flourish. Central Paris, if present trends continue, is fated to become a large-scale version of Venice, while the *banlieues* would be happy if they were able to turn into Venice's sprawling mainland offshoot, Mestre. Paris's success was also the source of its failure. The Grand Projets of President Mitterrand in the 1980s could only change the architectural language, not the basic structure of the French capital.

Haussmann did not just build boulevards. He dug the sewers that allowed Paris to escape from the scourge of cholera. The dispossessed of Paris had to pay a price. Haussmann's policies forced them out of the old city centre. Paris was a century and a half ahead of Rio, Shanghai and Mumbai in seeing the eviction of existing communities from the homes that they had occupied for a generation or two to life in bleak barrack-like blocks on the outer edges of the city, while wealthy speculators profited from their forced departure.

For those Brazilians who worried about the negative impact of the transformation of the dockside *favela* of Morro da Providência in Rio into the Porto Maravilha, the city's promised glittering new waterfront, spurred by Olympic preparations for 2016, the negative aspects of Haussmann's Paris provided a hint of what was to come with none of the positive qualities of his boulevards.

A city is, up to a point, the product of those who design and make its buildings. But it is also shaped by the engineers who lay out its sewers and plan its roads, by the lawyers who frame the statutes that govern its land tenure, by the political legislation that shapes its development, by the builders and the developers who attempt to profit from scarce land and from reliable income streams from long-term rentals. It is shaped by technological shifts and changes in patterns of social interactions.

Cities are formed as much by ideas as they are by things; in either case more often than not they are the product of unintended consequences. The car, which is clearly a thing rather than an idea, was meant to offer personal mobility rather than lead to the emergence of out-of-town shopping, toxic air pollution and traffic jams. The standard shipping container, also a thing, was meant to speed up loading and cut down handling costs and pilfering. It did all that, but, rather more dramatically, it also wiped out every upstream dock, wharf and warehouse in the world, and eventually resulted in Canary Wharf becoming London's second financial centre. The three-electrode vacuum tube, or thermionic valve as it is known in the United States, was developed as a switch and an amplifier. It has done more than either the car or the shipping container to change the urban world. It has made the world digital, with all that implies for the economy, for communications and the patterns of everyday life.

As for ideas that define cities: there are the urban theorists who believed in a rigid division between parts of a city designated for homes and those zoned for work; the modernists who wanted a *tabula rasa*; and the followers of Camillo Sitte, the nineteenth-century Austrian architect who understood the city as a sequence of visual and spatial experiences. He inspired those who wanted to give new suburbs the picturesque character of traditional villages. There are also some ideas less immediately obvious in their relevance to the nature of a city but which eventually have the biggest impact. These might be the legal codes

Hamburg and Detroit both had their origins as port cities. Detroit flourished briefly in the twentieth century as the heart of the modern car industry. Its collapse left its centre in ruins; its Michigan Theater became a car park (top). With older roots going back to the Hansa trading network, Hamburg has been more resilient, and built itself a new opera house (bottom) in the midst of a reconstructed harbour.

that result in certain kinds of leases, the political ideas about participation or centralization that impact on how decisions about what to build, and what not to build, are taken. And there are the fuel subsidies that may encourage one form of transport over another, and thus favour some forms of urbanism over others.

The steam-age city was soot-streaked and smog-bound. It depended for its mobility, its factories and its comfort on the begrimed stokers confined below ground and below deck whose back-breaking toil fed the boilers. Electricity seemed as far removed from this sweat-soaked reliance on muscle power as the digital economy is now from the analogue.

Electricity was always a thing too: a thing that has had a massive impact on the form and density of cities. Lifts, street lights, tramlines, air conditioning, neon and escalators changed the face of the first industrial metropolises. Berlin, London, New York and Chicago, as they are today, would not be possible without electricity, and not only in the physical sense but in their political organization too. Electricity made possible the technology that sidestepped literacy, and allowed politicians to speak directly to the masses 80 years ago. There is nothing new about the impact of technology on civic strife, whatever the claims made for the BlackBerry-fuelled mayhem in the streets of London's Hackney and Haringey during the riots of 2011 or for Twitter in the Arab Spring. Fifty years earlier it was the transistor radios that French conscripts carried in their backpacks that carried President de Gaulle's call for them to resist the orders of their mutinous officers in Colonial Algeria.

If cities really are the wealth-creating machines that we all need them to be, if they are to go on turning the poor into the not so poor, then their leaders are constantly faced with the challenge of what happens if the machine stops working. When the economy goes sour, when big employers lose their way or move out, if the city can't restart its engine, it finds itself drained of the productive and the talented who have the skills to move elsewhere, leaving those without such skills caught in a downward spiral of decline. There are troubles that can be brought by success too. When pollution runs out of control, even those who profit from it fear for the health of their own children. When property speculation makes a city unaffordable for the talented, it is effectively destroying the very qualities that have made it successful. It is this anxiety that is behind the febrile exchanges of ideas about urbanism which spread like viruses. Successful cities are determined to keep ahead of their competitors and are continually coming up with new ways in which they can do so. Less successful cities are constantly sending fact-finding delegations around the world to see what they can learn from others.

If Hong Kong, which successfully survived the loss of a million or more manufacturing jobs to mainland China when the Special Enterprise Zone at Shenzhen was set up, sees the next stage in its economic development as involving the construction of a new cultural complex in West Kowloon, then so does Singapore at the Esplanade. Both are city states that have made themselves prosperous through a similar series of steps, moving from low-cost manufacturing in the 1960s, to creating airlines and airports to add to their deep-water harbours in the 1970s. From that base, they moved into banking, followed in the 1980s by boosting education, and now the creative industries and culture. Because Singapore and Hong Kong are both seen as success stories, synonymous with the shape of the evolution of the city at the start of the twenty-first century, then Baku, Dubai and Abu Dhabi and half a dozen other ambitious cities want their own opera houses, their own museums and their own art biennales so that they can follow in their footsteps. Some of these ambitions are more successful than others.

The position of the Gulf States, midway between Europe and Asia, has encouraged them to make massive investments in airports and airlines. It has led to absurd overprovision within tight geographical confines for reasons of national prestige more than commercial logic. Despite all this, one or more of the contenders will succeed in building a hub that will reshape the world's transport routes. The culture-led approach for the Gulf is currently less convincing. There is little evidence that the Emirati public have much appetite for contemporary art of the kind collected by the Guggenheim, or are interested in visiting museums in the traditional European way.

A more modest version of the same phenomenon of the contagion of ideas is visible in the bicycles-for-hire scheme that began in Paris at the end of the 1990s. It spread to London, with two different mayors both claiming the credit, then Milan, Prague and even Melbourne got them too. Such schemes do not always translate well to local conditions. Melbourne is a city that likes to cycle, but imposes a legal requirement to wear a cycling helmet, which is not something that works well with the idea of an instant cycle-hire service. The congestion-charging policy adopted by London in 2003 to discourage commuting by car was inspired by what Singapore had already done. Despite Mayor Bloomberg's best attempts to take the idea to New York he could not bring his electorate with him.

Equally curious is the way that, for a moment, the cable car was considered the instant solution to the problems of the *barrios* of Medellín, an idea which quickly spread to Caracas, then Rio and La Paz. It was a presented as a cheap and rapid way of allowing the dispossessed from the slums access to the jobs available in more affluent downtowns that would otherwise be impossibly distant from the shacks perched on perilously steep slopes. It was repurposing technology developed for Alpine ski resorts, and the makers of the systems were only too eager to ship their products to rather less familiar users. In the case of the *favelas* of Rio, pacified by paramilitary squads of special police, it was not clear how much of the traffic was from cleaners and labourers taking the cable car down to the city centre to work, and how much was going the other way, made up of tourists looking for the thrill of a safari through territory controlled by the notorious gangs at minimal risk. Boris Johnson quixotically brought a single cable car route to London at the time of the 2012 Olympics, spanning the Thames between North Greenwich and the Royal Docks. It is now hardly used.

Cities are not static creations, they change and they develop. Slums take hold, though in the Western world they are now more likely to be in unfavoured suburbs rather than clustered around city centres. Old industries die, investment money comes in from all over the world to transform city centres, threatening long-established residents who are priced out of the neighbourhoods that they once knew.

To make sense of a city, you need to know something about the people who live in it, and the people who built it. You need to ask how they did it and why.

We value the quality of the unpredictable as one of the key virtues of the city. We want to get lost in cities, we don't want them to be comprehensible all at once. We want to discover them gradually, to understand their layers of complexity. It is what makes New York's grid such an unexpected experience for those familiar with the supposedly more organic, unstructured European city. What at first sight looks like the ruthless order and logic of Manhattan in fact allows every kind of energy to flourish.

We are caught with conflicting ways of understanding the cities in which we live, as we struggle to decide how best to regenerate them, and to prevent overdevelopment, while ensuring that Frank O'Hara can find his 'sign that people do not totally regret life' in the elusive urban qualities that are so important to us.

The Barcelona Olympics and the Bilbao Guggenheim still cast a long shadow. It was great for them, so why not for us, ask ambitious mayors everywhere.

But that is to present cities as the victims of a kind of cargo cult. In reality, it is not the cities that simply build museums in the hope that something will turn up that are the successes. The cities that succeed are the ones that are rooted in the kind of cultural climate that is creative enough to fill the museums as well as build them.

Chapter Two

How to Make a City

1. The Name

To make a city, the first thing you will need is a name to call it by. Any name can work, though some certainly suggest a more successful future than others. Chechnya's capital city is called Grozny, which translates from the Russian as 'fearsome'. It goes back to the name of the colonial fort that the Tsar established in Chechnya at the start of the nineteenth century, around which a city of what is now 271,000 people eventually grew. It is a name that certainly reflects Grozny's tortured history, from Stalin's genocidal mass deportations and Putin's murderous war to force it back into Russia's orbit, to its subsequent descent into warlordism. But it is not necessarily the kind of identity that attracts eager new citizens or investors.

Ramzan Kadyrov, Chechnya's current ruler, came to power when his father was killed by a separatist bomb in 2004. He is a man with a taste for tracksuits, gold chains, martial arts and building Moscow-funded skyscrapers. He keeps a pet tiger cub on a lead, and holds court with Gerard Depardieu and Mike Tyson.

A refugee camp erupting hopelessly in the midst of a war or a natural catastrophe has no name. The sense of purpose that can eventually turn a settlement, even one born in the most difficult circumstances, into a city begins when it acquires a name. In 1630, a group of English Puritans fleeing religious persecution at home left for North America and named what would some day be a city of three million after Boston, the town in England that they had left behind. Tel Aviv was founded in 1909 by a handful of refugees displaced by European pogroms. They gathered on a beach outside Jaffa, drew lots for sites on which to build homes, and gave the land a Hebrew name.

Slums are different. Mostly, they do have names, even if they were acquired with random promiscuity, but it doesn't lead to investment or permanence. The lack of infrastructure is limiting.

One name that attached itself to a city in this way is Complexo do Alemão, the violent Rio de Janeiro *favela* that started to grow faster and faster from 1950 onwards. More or less illegally it has spilled breeze blocks and corrugated asbestos cement roof tiles over every inch of the land that was once owned by an immigrant referred to by the first squatters as the 'Alemão', Portuguese for 'German'. 'Alemão' is also the faintly dismissive term in Brazil for any fair-skinned foreigner, and the particular foreigner who owned Complexo do Alemão had actually been born in Poland rather than Germany.

Another randomly acquired name is that of Soweto, the bleak city on the edge of Johannesburg that grew, equally bleakly, out of the English acronym for South Western Townships.

Soweto has its roots in a settlement process that is very different from the shanty towns of Brazil. It is the product of an attempt by the vanished apartheid regime to force black people out of those city-centre areas that it designated for whites. In Complexo do Alemão, life is also lawless, short and harsh. But it is a community initiated by the people who live in it rather than a settlement that was imposed on them. Its homes look like random accretions, clinging like barnacles to a rock, rather than the tidy ranks of single-storey breeze-block houses with pitched roofs that are the product of Soweto's penal master plan. One, in Christopher Alexander's words, could be described as natural, and the other as artificial. All the same, the heavily armed pacification squads that invaded the *favelas* in the run-up to the Rio Olympics made the Complexo do Alemão look as though it was under military occupation. They showed some discipline, unlike the police death squads that have operated in other parts of Brazil.

A city sometimes reflects the act of will of the individual who brought it into being. Alexander the Great named Alexandria for himself. Scarcely less immodestly, Peter the Great gave St

Peter the Great established St Petersburg to tilt Russia towards Europe, using Amsterdam as a model and Italian architects to realize his vision. He is commemorated by an equestrian statue (above).

Chapter Two

Tel Aviv, born in 1909 when its founding families gathered on a beach overlooking the Mediterranean to allocate building plots (above), has no landmark to match that of St Petersburg.

After more than a century Tel Aviv has gone from a Bauhaus transplant to a high-rise city on the beach.

Chapter Two

Brasília was a political foundation: the affirmation of a nation that turned its back on the country's coastal, colonial cities. Its monumental architecture set out a claim to modernity.

The green spaces of Brasília's city centre have little relationship with its suburbs in which most of its people live. Yet it does provide an unforgettable image of urbanism.

Petersburg the name of his patron saint. George Washington chose the location of the US capital but not the name. That came as a tribute from the commissioners put in charge of the construction of the US capital by Congress.

When Juscelino Kubitschek surprised his electorate, and perhaps even himself, by carrying out the provisions of the Brazilian constitution and building a new capital within his five-year term in office as president, he named it for his country.

In 1967 the British government decided to call a new city of 250,000 people, that it planned to build along the route of the M1 motorway halfway between London and Birmingham, Milton Keynes. This was not an attempt to couple the author of *Paradise Lost* with the twentieth-century economist, as if in some earnest effort to erode the line between culture and science. Nor was it capitalism's riposte to Karl-Marx-Stadt, as the East German city of Chemnitz was called between 1953 and 1990. In fact, Milton Keynes was the name of a Buckinghamshire village that was about to be engulfed by the new city. The village died, but its name lives on in the entity that extinguished it. Ancient lanes and Georgian brick houses still survive in the midst of Milton Keynes, trapped among the precast concrete terraces, the business parks and the traffic-segregating underpasses.

Cities with contested identities come with multiple names. To use one rather than another – Derry rather than Londonderry, for example – is to demonstrate a particular interpretation of the city's history. When the names of cities are changed for political reasons, outcomes can be unpredictable. Mumbai's English speakers, for the most part members of an Indian intellectual elite, are much more likely to use the old name of Bombay than their British counterparts, who may be overcompensating for past offence.

Mumbai's roots go back to the successive waves of the European colonization of India. The Portuguese handed over the cluster of islands and fishing villages that constituted Bombay to the British in the seventeenth century. The 20,000 inhabitants of those days have swelled to an estimated 18 million, as a port city successively became a mill complex, a railway hub, a financial centre, and a centre for the Indian cinema industry. Its architectural expression ranges from the hallucinogenic translation of High Victorian Gothic from England to the subcontinent of the Chhatrapati Shivaji railway terminus, designed by F. W. Stevens with the swagger of St Pancras in London, to Charles Correa's high-rise apartments that synthesize modernism with India's climate. More recently the feverish skyscraper palace built by American architects Perkins+Will, for Mukesh Ambani, son of an enormously wealthy self-made billionaire, and his family, shamelessly delineates individual wealth on the skyline of the city. Water and power supplies are erratic, the suburban railway network is so overcrowded that commuters hanging from open doors are killed every day. There are 300,000 street vendors in Mumbai, just a few thousand of them are licensed. The rest are subject to continual insecurity and even those who are licensed can still be moved on by the police at any time.

It is a situation that encourages a pervasive climate of corruption. Mumbai's slums are of two kinds: the authorized, for which the municipal authority has a responsibility to provide basic services; and the unauthorized, which are subject to demolition, and where there is no duty by the city to provide power or water. There are impossible densities. Dharavi, the largest of the city's slums, packs up to 1,800 people into an acre. London's inner city plans for 136 people to the acre, but London's most densely populated borough, Islington, is seven times the size of Dharavi, but is home to 200,000 people, while Dharavi has an estimated one million. Authorized slums such as Dharavi are outnumbered by the 60 per cent that are illegal. Some of the illegals rely on unauthorized standpipes; a few have no water at all. The run-up to municipal elections in the city sees some unauthorized slums being strategically authorized, so that local politicians can create useful banks of grateful voters to support them, but they are not yet seen as permanent enough, in the eyes of the city, to develop into suburbs or towns.

Some cities measure out their histories in multiple identities, throwing light on to the varying political and cultural agendas of their leaders. Istanbul, once called Constantinople, and before that Byzantium, has been the capital city of three different empires. It is shaped by the surviving fragments of the Greek, Roman, Byzantine and Ottoman civilizations that built it. Archaeologists monitor every building project in the city centre. The railway tunnel under the Bosphorus linking Asia with Europe was held up for four years while the remains of a fleet of Byzantine ships were carefully excavated, documented and preserved. The attempted redevelopment of Taksim Square was delayed even before the Gezi Park protests by the possible presence of Genoese tombs and fifth-century sarcophagi. Istanbul is a place in which to sit under the shade of ancient olive trees for a leisurely afternoon, watching the sun on the water of the Bosphorus from the terrace of the Sabancı Museum. Like so many cultural institutions in the city, the museum is privately owned; established by one of the handful of wealthy families that dominate Turkey's economy. It's a memory of the way that New York worked in the nineteenth century, although the plutocrats there built coalitions between themselves to establish civic institutions jointly. In Istanbul things are still too competitive for that to have happened yet. The Sabancı shows Picasso paintings and Ottoman calligraphy. Its restaurant, which is much favoured by the editors of *Wallpaper* magazine, is in contemporary Scandinavian style with a menu shaped by a chef from New Zealand. For those with a taste for something grittier, there is Istanbul Modern, a gallery funded by the Eczacıbaşı family on a site with an even better view across the Bosphorus. It is housed in one of a series of concrete-framed dockside sheds from the 1960s. A graceful, early-nineteenth-century mosque built in the Italianate manner stands immediately behind it. Another of Turkey's financial dynasties, the Koç family, maintains its own museum, this one devoted to transport, further along the waterfront.

Istanbul is the city in which Roger Short, the British Consul General, and 29 other people perished and another 400 were injured when a truck bomb slammed into the stone gateposts of Sir Charles Barry's classical consulate building, which was once the British embassy to the Sublime Porte, as the Ottoman court was known, at a moment in 2003 when George Bush was in London talking to Tony Blair.

Istanbul is the city in which Ragip Zarakolu was jailed for five months for insulting the Turkish republic by publishing a book written by a British author that questioned the country's treatment of its Armenian minority. It's where Hrant Dink, the Armenian journalist, was assassinated for his political views. It's the point of departure for western recruits for ISIS and a battleground between Kurdish militants and the Turkish police.

Although modern Turkey's founder, Kemal Atatürk, was born in what is now Greece, he moved his capital from Istanbul in European Turkey to Ankara in Asia, a city created from almost nothing. He insisted on Istanbul as the name for what much of the rest of the world continued to call Constantinople. In Slav languages it was known as Tsarigrad, a name that is still used in Bulgaria. Iceland has its own name for Istanbul that goes back to the time of the eleventh-century Viking raids on the Black Sea, when they referred to it as simply the 'Great City'. From 1930 onwards, the Turkish post office has refused to deliver mail addressed to any other version of the name for the city than Istanbul.

The more historic trading connections, the more linguistic variations there are for a city's name. The more powerful the city, the more likely all its trading partners will be to use its common name.

For the first few decades of modern Turkey's existence, the state poured resources into the new capital, which had just

28,000 people in 1924. Atatürk's ambitious building programmes made it seem as if Ankara would eventually overtake Istanbul. But as Turkey urbanized, Istanbul shot ahead of Ankara. Its population of more than one million at the end of the First World War slumped to 600,000 after Atatürk moved the capital and the Greeks and Armenians either left or were killed. It has quadrupled since 1980 to almost 13 million. The population figures give Istanbul a strong claim to be regarded as the largest city in Europe, even if it lies partly in Asia, where a third of its citizens live. The collapse of the Soviet Union helped Istanbul prosper by providing services and expertise to the energy-rich former Soviet republics. Istanbul was the base for the architects, the construction companies, the advertising agencies and the banks that reshaped Kazakhstan, Azerbaijan and Ukraine. Rising tensions with Vladimir Putin's Russia led to the abrupt termination of many of those contracts.

Istanbul was meant to be Turkey's passport into the European Union: a sophisticated First World enclave in a country that has honour killings and an ongoing, not always low-intensity, war with its Kurds. Then all semblance of order on its borders with Syria and Iraq collapsed and the country faced a crisis between the secular and the Islamists, and between the president and his former Islamist allies led by Fethullah Gülen, the exiled Sunni preacher. It is a fractured city. In the suburb of Levent, on the European side of the city where banks cluster, you can find facsimiles of smart London restaurants in the Kanyon shopping centre designed by the American master of the mall, Jon Jerde. But Istanbul is also a place where Orhan Pamuk, Turkey's only winner of the Nobel Prize for Literature, suggests that on some streets you will find the blood of ritually slaughtered sheep running in the gutters on holy days.

The rural poor, who tend to religious orthodoxy, have moved

Modern Turkey is defined by two cities – Istanbul, which Kemal Atatürk asked Henri Prost (top), to transform into a westernised city – and Ankara, that he made into a national capital after the collapse of the Ottoman Empire. Atatürk's mausoleum, (bottom) remains a point of conflict between securalists and Islamists.

Chapter Two

Henri Prost's remodeling of Istanbul involved the demolition of an Ottoman barracks (above), to make way for Gezi Park. President Erdoğan's attempts to destroy the park and rebuild the barracks to overturn Atatürk's city provoked weeks of civil unrest.

Named for Atatürk, Istanbul's cultural centre is an architectural landmark with a contested political meaning. Erdoğan wants to destroy it, and all it stands for. Turkey's secularists see it as a defining symbol of their national identity.

to Istanbul in growing numbers since 1955, when the city had just 1.5 million people, changing the character of Turkey's most cosmopolitan city. Those parts of the city in which non-Turkish ethnic groups and faiths other than Islam were once tolerated now coexist uneasily with areas that have become the heartland of a more conservative constituency. There are empty Greek schools, a few synagogues still hanging on, and perhaps 100 functioning churches left.

Istanbul is a city in which the mayor's wife now wears the headscarf that Turkey's judges prohibited from university campuses and government buildings for eight decades as antithetical to the secularist constitution. The increasingly authoritarian President Recep Tayyip Erdoğan has overturned the ban, and is attempting to introduce 'modest' dress codes and restrict the sale of alcohol.

In some parts of the city, Kemalist local administrations still fill walls with portraits of the founder of modern Turkey. In other, Islamist areas, the streets are being renamed after Ottoman generals. It is a city whose contemporary meaning is continually being adjusted and manipulated for political ends.

Hagia Sophia, for almost a millennium the supreme church of Orthodox Christianity, was turned into a mosque when the Ottomans conquered the city over 500 years ago. The addition of a ring of minarets signalled the change, along with inscriptions in Arabic, and the suppression of Christian iconography. In the 1930s, at the height of Atatürk's modernization drive, the mosque became a museum. In the last decade, there have been increasingly strident demands from Islamists to turn the museum back into a mosque. These successive incarnations reflect the contested meanings of Istanbul that some people are ready to kill to impose.

2. The Monuments

Cities with contested identities have their names changed. The way in which the monuments that serve to define those meanings are erased and recreated reflects the course of the conflict. In 2013, Gezi Park on the edge of Taksim Square became the flashpoint between two bitterly opposed views of what Istanbul should be. When the bulldozers went in to uproot the park, first Istanbul and then all liberal Turkey erupted in protest. On one level, this was characterized as a crude onslaught on civilized urbanism, an egregious collaboration between politicians and well-connected property developers. The park and Taksim Square beyond it were occupied night after night by protestors. There was more to this than a row between property developers and a group of eco-activists determined to keep a green space from disappearing under a shopping mall.

It was a battle in the proxy war for control of Turkey's identity. Gezi Park was created in the years between 1933 and 1940 after Atatürk and Lütfi Kirdar, the Mayor of Istanbul at the time, commissioned the French planner Henri Prost to modernize the city. Prost's project for Istanbul was an essential part of Atatürk's determination to redefine Turkey as a secular state. He had already imported a Viennese architect to plan Ankara as a modern capital. Atatürk abolished the Arabic script and created a new Latin alphabet for the Turkish language.

Modernization in those days meant making Istanbul appear as Western as possible. Atatürk's Turkey went looking for the best available talent to deliver that ambition. Prost was one of the most distinguished planners of his generation. He was responsible for shaping the growth of Greater Paris in the 1920s. Before he moved to Istanbul, he had worked extensively in French-controlled Morocco on the development of Tangier, Marrakech and Fez.

In North Africa, Prost laid out administrative and commercial centres with regular French-style street plans. He preserved the distinctive character of the medinas and the souks, though they became more or less picturesque adjuncts to the new centres to which power subsequently migrated.

It was different in Turkey. Prost wanted historic Istanbul to remain as the heart of a restructured city. He set about protecting the monuments of Rome and Byzantium, but cleared away the Ottoman accretions around them to create new streets and public spaces. He believed he was giving the past a better setting.

Gezi Park, which he described as the start of Istanbul's version of the Bois de Boulogne, was one of his principle creations. He planned to connect it to the rest of the city with grand boulevards like the ones that Haussmann cut through the centre of Paris.

To make way for the park, Prost demolished a monumental artillery barracks, built in the orientalist style in 1806. Erdoğan and his Islamist followers want to bring back the Istanbul that Atatürk did his best to wipe out. For Erdoğan the loss of the Ottoman empire that once stretched from Mecca in the south and Baku in the east, to Algiers in the west and Budapest in the north is as much of a tragedy and is as keenly felt as the collapse of the Soviet Union is by Vladimir Putin. For both men, restoring at least the symbols of what has gone, if not all of its substance, has become a consuming passion. Erdoğan has embarked on a massive mosque-building programme, which is not confined to Turkey. For political reasons, he has funded mosques in many former Ottoman territories, including Albania, Macedonia and Kosovo.

Erdoğan has drawn opposition even from pious Muslims for his plans to construct an enormous new mosque on the Asian side of Istanbul, on the Çamlica Hill, which they describe as a cheap copy of the Blue Mosque. He has named the third Bosphorus bridge for Selim the Implacable, the most expansionist of the Ottoman emperors.

In Ankara he has built a huge presidential palace to reflect his attempt to transform what was once the purely titular nature of the Turkish head of state into an executive role. Istanbul's new airport, planned to be the world's largest with six runways and an eventual capacity of 150 million a year, will be named for Erdoğan himself. In an entirely deliberate gesture, the existing Atatürk Airport will be closed when its replacement opens. While the state is investing massively in infrastructure, metro systems, high-speed railways and new bridges that suggest a continuation of Atatürk's modernizing mission, at Taksim Square, Erdoğan has insisted on the reappearance of the ghost of the barracks that the first modernizers demolished in 1938. Its second coming, if it happens, will not be as a military installation, but as a shopping centre. Few things, on the face of it, are as secular as a shopping mall but, for Erdoğan, form is apparently as significant as content. The building of a shopping mall to look like an Ottoman barracks is the architectural version of the attempts of Erdoğan's acolytes in the Turkish national airline to dress female flight attendants in Ottoman-inspired coat dresses and the fez.

After three increasingly tense weeks and 11 deaths, Erdoğan withdrew the riot police and paused his destruction of Gezi Park. He turned his attention to the Atatürk Cultural Centre, one of Turkey's principle modern landmarks facing the park on the side of Taksim Square. Designed in the 1960s it housed the national opera company and a concert hall. It closed in 2008, and the Sabancı family announced four years later that it would pay for its reconstruction. Güler Sabancı explained that:

> The Atatürk Cultural Centre [designed by Hayati Tabanlioğlu] is of the utmost historical significance and value. It is a structure that symbolizes republican values. The Atatürk

> Cultural Centre constitutes a very significant place in our hearts, in the art and culture events of the republican history and in our beloved Taksim. We are grateful that we can contribute to preserve a symbol of republican values for art lovers, staying faithful to the original yet with new technologies.

Restoration work still hasn't started. After the shock of the failed coup in the summer of 2016, and the waves of repression that have followed, most likely it never will. During the Gezi protests, the building became a temporary base for riot police. Then Erdoğan announced that he would have it torn down and replaced by yet another mosque, perhaps in an effort to face down the religious followers of Fethullah Gülen as well as the secularists. Atatürk's monument is still standing so far, albeit lost behind a layer of advertising hoardings.

Other cities also have buildings like Istanbul's barracks, which shape memories long after their physical traces have been erased. The basilica of Christ the Saviour was built under the Kremlin's walls to celebrate Russian victory over Napoleon. Part of the cost was met with money raised by donations of a few kopeks each from peasants all across Russia. Tchaikovsky wrote the 1812 Overture to celebrate its completion in 1880. With its massive domes visible from across the Moscow River it was both a landmark that helped to define Moscow's urban landscape, and an institution at the heart of its civic life. It was an assertion of national pride: the largest Orthodox church in the world, filling the gap left by the Islamisation of Hagia Sophia.

Stalin demolished the basilica in 1931, and cleared the site to make room for the Palace of the Soviets to create another history for the city. He jailed those few devout priests who were prepared to risk their lives to protect the church from demolition. Stalin ordered the dynamiting of the building to demonstrate his version of the city's identity. Religion had to be brought under

Moscow's most highly charged urban site after the Kremlin is the Basilica of Christ the Saviour. Built to celebrate Russia's defeat of Napoleon, Stalin blew it up to make way for the Palace of the Soviets: an assertion of the atheist, socialist state (overleaf).

Khruschev ended Stalinism by turning the site of the Palace of the Soviets (left) into a huge outdoor swimming pool (top). Post-socialist Russia signalled yet another new political order by recreating the lost basilica (above).

control and rendered harmless. His architect for the Palace of the Soviets, Boris Iofan, chosen in competition ahead of Le Corbusier and Walter Gropius, faithfully followed his master's instructions and came up with a design as tall as the Empire State Building, topped by a colossal representation of Lenin on the scale of the Statue of Liberty gesturing towards the future. In a twist of fate too unlikely to make plausible fiction, Iofan the Stalinist had previously worked in Rome for Armando Brasini, the fascist architect who planned Mussolini's settlements in Libya. The Palace of the Soviets would have been 500 metres high, the Vatican of Marxism–Leninism, the tallest building in Russia by far, and a structure that would have dominated every view of Moscow. Construction got as far as the ninth floor before the Nazi invasion of the Soviet Union put a stop to it. Work restarted fitfully after the war, and was finally abandoned only after Stalin's death in 1953. During the hungriest years of the purges and the Great Patriotic War, Stalin's propagandists used images of the Palace of the Soviets to fill the windows of Moscow's empty shops with a vision of the eventual triumph of the regime. Nikita Khrushchev, Stalin's successor, destroyed the surviving fragments of the palace in a kind of exorcism of his predecessor and his hold over the Soviet Union. In its place he built a giant open-air swimming pool that became a pleasure ground for Muscovites hoping for better times.

The fall of the Soviet Union, and the Marxist ideology to which it paid at least nominal allegiance, created a vacuum eagerly filled by nationalism and the Orthodox Church, with which Russian nationalism is closely identified. Even before the collapse of the old system the state had given permission for the church to be rebuilt. The first post-Soviet Mayor of Moscow, Yuri Luzhkov, demolished the pool and began to build a replica of what Stalin had destroyed. The lavish gold leaf on the domes was funded by gifts from the new generation of the wealthy, the oligarchs. It is the church in which the five members of Pussy Riot filmed their

40-second protest against the connections between Putin and the Orthodox Church. It is also where Boris Yeltsin lay in state.

Stalin set an example that he encouraged his German subjects to follow. After his puppet government took power in the German Democratic Republic, it destroyed the symbolic heart of Imperial Germany, Berlin's Hohenzollern Palace, which had been abandoned by the Kaiser and his family when they were exiled in the closing days of the First World War. Russia had slightly different symbolic priorities. The Tsar and his family were slaughtered, but his palaces survived even if many of Russia's historic places of worship did not.

Berlin's baroque palace, built between the fifteenth and eighteenth centuries, was dynamited for much the same reasons that Stalin blew up the basilica: to destroy the symbolic heart of Imperial Germany as he had destroyed the symbolic heart of Russia's Christian identity. In Berlin, only the balcony from which the martyred Communist leader Karl Liebknecht proclaimed the Spartacist Revolution and the birth of a new republic in 1919 survived as a fragment trapped in the shoddy glass façade of the new Foreign Ministry. Ostensibly, the DDR did not have the resources to invest in restoring a redundant imperialist relic. In fact, the destruction of the palace was a signal by the Party that there would be no going back to the old order. This was the capital of a new Germany, the Western version of the city was the anomaly and it was socialism that was here to stay. The site of the palace was cleared of rubble in the early days of the Cold War. The Party faithful celebrated May Day with elaborate parades staged just a few metres from the square in which Nazi students had once burned the books that they disapproved of. Later, the East Germans invested in their bronze-glass and white-marble toy parliament, the Palast der Republik, to show that West Berlin did not have a monopoly on civic glamour.

After reunification, the Palast, which was completed only in 1976, became superfluous to the requirements of a new Germany.

Despite having been the place in which the East voted for democracy, and the warm memories that many East Berliners still had of it as a place for an evening at the discotheque or the bowling alley that it accommodated alongside its debating chamber, it was marked for demolition. For a while it was used as a space for contemporary art installations, until sufficient asbestos was found inside to justify its final destruction. Against the protests of more liberal-minded Berliners, a well-organized campaign agitated for Germany to recreate the lost palace. Angela Merkel eventually agreed to fund the building of something that looked like the old palace, with its dome, classical masonry and multiple courtyards. Much like Istanbul's artillery barracks, quite what this hulking structure would be used for was less of an issue than recreating a facsimile of the building that had once served to define Berlin. For some, the £600 million reconstruction seemed like a worrying, and worryingly costly, piece of historical revisionism.

German intellectual curiosity eventually reasserted itself. The palace was renamed the Humboldtforum in the summer of 2011. It's a name that tactfully manages to refer both to Berlin's nineteenth-century glory, when Wilhelm von Humboldt was one of the founders of the city's first university, and the DDR, which renamed that university for Humboldt and his brother, Alexander. The forum has a triumvirate of curators, chaired by Neil MacGregor, formerly of the British Museum, to give it an intellectual direction for its new role as a cultural centre alongside the Museum Island, where Prussia's monumental cultural landmarks have been carefully restored.

In Berlin, as in Moscow and Istanbul, landmarks have defined the identity of the city in a symbolic sense. Monuments are the part of its fabric that most represents a city. On a pragmatic level they are the fixed points by which people orientate themselves. They define the emotional life of a city, and they are the physical record of its history.

3. People and resources

After its name and its monuments, if a city is going to grow, it needs people. If you are Alexander the Great, or President Kubitschek responsible for building Brasília, the leaders of the Burmese Junta, the founders of the United States, or Kemal Atatürk, you can count on your retainers, your civil servants, your judiciary, your army and your politicians to come. But that is a limited group, unlikely to bring a city to life.

The carpetbaggers, the priests, the hoteliers, the bartenders and the brothel-keepers who are always early arrivals in a new city add yeast to the mix. The other service industries follow. Once it was the fencing instructors, the dancing masters and the wig-makers, now it is the consultants and the art advisers, the ultra-high-net-worth-individual bankers and the life coaches.

Provided that you can give them a place to live and work in, the food, the water and power to sustain them, the law and order to protect them, the rest will come. There are examples of places where they didn't, because some of the basics of life were missing. Fatehpur Sikri, for example, a city of red-sandstone pavilions, was the capital of Moghul India for little more than a decade until it died of thirst. When it ran out of water the Moghul court moved to Lahore.

As Roman Polanski's cinematic masterpiece *Chinatown* shows so powerfully, water is at the heart of every city, a resource that is fought over, invested in, misused and cherished. Polanski's film is set against the background of the California water wars of the early twentieth century when a private aqueduct was built to divert supplies from the Owens Valley. Control of water is still essential to the survival of the logic-defying spread of Los Angeles's furthest-flung settlements, where commuting times run into hours and where the water supply is increasingly uncertain. To secure its water needs, its boundaries spread as far as Colorado, if not politically then at least in terms of spheres of influence. If it loses that water, Los Angeles's endless suburbs, built far into the deserts inland of the city, have no future.

Without water, cities die in the way that Fatehpur Sikri expired. It's a fate that could yet befall the Gulf city states with their glittering instant skylines, their airports, their burgeoning cultural centres and their skyscrapers. They depend on desalination plants burning hydrocarbons to produce not just drinking water but also the water that Abu Dhabi uses, with breathtaking profligacy, to feed the grass embankments on its urban roads. That desalination is in itself damaging the coastal ecosystem.

The Emiratis have already paid for their new homes in London, Paris and New York, ready for the day when their cities become uninhabitable and they are able to leave behind a cluster of abandoned football stadia, derelict museums and forests of empty towers. It took the once-guano-rich island of Nauru just a single decade to go through this process, propelling its citizens from poverty to riches and back. The Gulf will take longer: its governments are better advised and they are preparing for the future. But it could still happen.

It is water that keeps all cities alive. Water makes possible their sewage systems, and defines their boundaries. Without a water supply, a city stops growing. Cities that seek to control a scarce water supply will try to annex the land on which it depends. It is water in the form of rivers and harbours that brings cities the trade in goods and the people that make them flourish.

It is also water that in so many cases shapes the character of a city. Dickens reflected on the special qualities of light that the Thames gives London. A river can connect different parts of a city, but also divide them. For centuries the Thames was a psychological as well as a physical barrier dividing a regulated north bank from a more lawless south. As a result, the Southwark of

Shakespeare's time had something of the character of Ciudad Juárez, on the Mexican side of the Rio Grande from El Paso. In both cases residents of the more prosperous north of the divide had a tendency to cross the river for illicit purposes. The centuries-long division between north and south in London has only begun to dissipate in the last two decades.

It is public investment in communal facilities, of which water is the most essential, that has served to shape the evolution of municipal government and establish the complex financing mechanisms that define their tax base. Throughout urban history waterborne sewage systems and reservoirs from Constantinople to Los Angeles, built out of massive stone or in reinforced concrete, have represented some of the most impressive physical manifestations of urbanism. The responses of cities to climate and landscape, which range from the dependence of Minneapolis on underground passageways for pedestrians to help them survive harsh winters, to the natural air-cooling forms of traditional Arab architecture, are the physical manifestations of urban forms to place and environment.

Capital cities are special cases. They are the firstborn of the urban family, spoiled and cosseted, looked upon both jealously and dismissively by those who live elsewhere. A capital is the privileged home of a unique set of institutions, shaped by symbolic values and allowed first call on national resources. City states are different, more like infant prodigies: equipped either with an enormous brain or a vast fortune in natural resources, but vulnerable when the neighbourhood bully turns nasty or when, like London, they come out on the wrong side of a national referendum. And then there are the second cities. Within the gravitational orbit of a nation state, cities form part of a solar system that provides a kind of hierarchy, often in the sense of pairings.

The history of Quebec, for example, has been determined by the relationship between outward-looking Montreal and the nationalists of Quebec City, just as Scotland is a culture polarized between Glasgow, with its global outlook based on trade and industry, and Edinburgh, home of Scotland's legal, political and religious institutions. There is another kind of tension visible in the divide between Barcelona and Madrid, between Beijing and Shanghai, and between Sydney and Melbourne. They are city pairs that compete for investment, jobs, and for prestige within a national and international context. They all want the hub airport, the stock exchange, the elite university and the television station. They are probably not as interested in attracting the server farms that maintain the web, which may be important pieces of digital infrastructure but bring few jobs.

A city grows because it has the potential to be a wealth-creating machine for turning the poor into the not so poor. Selling shoelaces from a plastic bag at an illegal minibus stop at the edge of one of Johannesburg's townships, or Chinese-made toys from the pavement in Mexico City's Zócalo, is infinitely precarious, but it is still more secure than subsistence farming in drought-hit South Sudan or planting a smallholding in Chiapas in the face of narco-terrorists. Some come to the city because they are would-be entrepreneurs, others because they are desperate. Authoritarian states, of which Russia and China are the most populous, attempt, with increasing ineffectiveness, to discourage their citizens from moving from one city to another, or from the countryside to the cities. Yet the poor but ambitious in China or Russia are no less determined than the Nicaraguans trying to cross the Rio Grande into the United States, or the Syrians waiting in squalor at Calais in the hope that one day they might breach the Channel Tunnel's defences and reach England. Cities flourish when they can attract people, not when they have to come, but because they *want* to. They come because cities offer people the chance to live better lives than they could have elsewhere. From selling shoelaces, there is the chance to move on, to fund a stall, and then a shop. In time there may be enough left over from their earnings at the end of the week to send children to school, and for the family to find a place to live in a better part of the city.

Not all cities can rely on willing or even desperate newcomers. In fact, some fragile cities need to attract anyone they can. In those societies that allow their citizens the freedom to make a choice about where they live, they are subject to all the techniques of persuasion. Milton Keynes spent a lot of money putting its message on giant billboards across London in the 1990s. One of them read, in very large letters rendered in the manner of a neon motel sign, 'SORRY. THIS CITY IS FULL', and then, in very small ones, 'Move to Milton Keynes'. The corporation bought television advertising time to portray the pleasures of fishing in the canals of the new city, and to show a celebration of life in Milton Keynes with a three-minute clip that was a shameless steal from Albert Lamorisse's charming short film *Le Ballon Rouge*. One of the corporation's posters declared 'Milton Keynes will be good for your health'. Another poster showed three generations of hands: one larger, and clearly male, behind a smaller, presumably female, hand with painted fingernails, and a still smaller child's hand in front. 'Milton Keynes: The kind of city you'll want your family to grow up in', it boasted mawkishly. This is publicity of a kind that is a direct descendant of the fancifully engraved prospectuses produced by eighteenth-century hucksters attempting to sell swamps in the midst of Florida as plots of prime residential real estate to gullible Europeans with the benefit of city plans suggesting that grand boulevards and handsome monuments were already in place.

Coming to terms with the evolving nature of the contemporary city means facing up to the reality of the extraordinary scale shift of the later years of the twentieth century. Many cities now have populations far larger than those of entire European nations. A city with an effective population of 15 or 40 million is an entity with no historical precedent. We have no long-term experience of how such a city can operate.

We do have examples of much smaller cities losing their sense of cohesion and identity. It is a phenomenon that might be called the Balkanization of the city. Berlin was cut in two, leaving both sides so far apart for 40 years that the trauma has still not entirely healed. Beirut became three or more zones. Belfast and Sarajevo were cut into shreds, each fragment with its own social geography. In Belfast's case, the old centre was shared neutral territory common to warring factions. In other cases, the divided communities made the suburbs shared ground.

Some cities stubbornly maintain their own identity, even as they merge physically with others. The Randstad, or 'Edge City' as the Dutch call the megalopolis formed of the country's four biggest cities, for example, is less than the sum of its parts, mainly because even as Amsterdammers take the train to their jobs in Rotterdam every weekday, and remain in sight of a continuous ribbon of concrete for most of the journey, they never for a moment lose their sense of themselves as citizens of Amsterdam. And the same is true for the countless thousands of residents of Rotterdam making the journey in the opposite direction. They live in what is effectively a single city 40 miles long. But, bound by the tribalism of football loyalties, primary schools, the newspaper that they read, the bar they drink in, Rotterdammers know exactly who they are, just as Amsterdam is equally united in its unshakable conviction that it is anything but Rotterdam. And the identity of a city is not itself a monolithic one, but is subject to subdivision: north or south of the river, East or West End, bridge and tunnel or downtown. The identity of a city is the product of a complex set of attributes that build up over time and serve to define it. They differentiate one city from another; they reveal who belongs and who does not. One fundamental is the constant fluctuation of speech patterns and accents, reflecting how the rules and signals of belonging shift over time. Those who know the signs recognize that the Dutch spoken in Rotterdam is noticeably different to the version of Dutch that is spoken in Amsterdam, even though these are physically, if not administratively or culturally, to all intents and purposes a single entity. The Berlin version of German is less elaborate and less formal than the academic form of the language. Many words are pronounced differently in the capital, and as a result Berlin German sounds somehow more urbane than the standard version.

The particular obsession with class of the English makes their country especially tuned to the specific social implications of speech patterns. These are now as much signifiers of a city as of a social class. The term 'cockney' supposedly has its roots in the derision of sixteenth-century rural England for the overprotected urban fops of the time. It became the name for the definitive voice of working-class London, distilling with some precision a particular way of life at the start of the twentieth century. The accent has survived the dispersion of the communities that once lived in the east and south of the city into Essex and Kent, and even the humiliation of Hollywood's attempts to replicate it on screen, which have often seemed like parodies. When people speak a standard form of the language of others fluently, they impress their listeners. When they speak with a distinct local accent, they make them laugh. Cockney is not exactly a language, but it has changed and adapted over time, absorbing elements of the way that newcomers to the city speak. There have been traces of Jewish or Yiddish words in cockney for more than a century and now the rhythms of the Caribbean are making themselves felt. For a certain kind of Londoner, an accent is an assertion of their character in the face of the world's hostility. The football cults of the 1970s were as deliberately provocative as the punks. Both were a celebration of their status as undesirables to a more squeamish society.

Cockney usages have spread beyond London through television soaps, a cultural form that is now a mainstay of social anthropology. London patois has also been quick to absorb other influences, taking and giving, back and forth, with other cultures. Some spread through face-to-face contact, others through the media. The Metropolitan Police, whose officers were once known as 'coppers', a term exported to the US, were described by the time of London's Tottenham riots of 2011 as 'da Feds', through the ingestion of a surfeit of American gangsta rap, much as British education has absorbed the idea of the American high-school prom, and Guy Fawkes has been supplanted by Halloween. In the same way, middle-class Parisian children now use words derived from Arab usage inspired by the occupants of the *banlieues* descended from Algerian grandparents.

Cities have accommodated ethnically diverse groups almost from their beginnings along the Tigris and Euphrates in Mesopotamia 26 centuries or more before Christ. Ur, Alexandria and Rome all had communities from throughout the empires that built them. In the ruins of most classical cities you can find quarters that were once inhabited by Jews, next to Greek and Latin areas.

It is this cosmopolitanism which means that a city can offer a more inclusive sense of belonging than a nation state. To call yourself a Londoner, a New Yorker or a Muscovite is different from describing yourself as English, British, American or Russian. London has existed for far longer, after all, than anything that could remotely be described as England. It was established as a strategic river crossing by the Roman invaders nearly 2,000 years ago, at a time when the British isles were a patchwork of independent Celtic kingdoms. And it has successively been important for Roman Britain, for the Anglo-Saxons, Normans, for England and now for Britain.

Such multi-ethnicity can also break down from time to time.

The intercommunal violence that horrifyingly emerges from the slums of Mumbai or Delhi every so often is only a more intense version of the riots, looting and murders that swept Los Angeles in the wake of the Rodney King affair. Among the big cities of the modern world it is only Tokyo that remains a racially homogenous city, with little more than a hidden Korean community as the only major part of the population that is not ethnically Japanese. For a millennium it has been perhaps the only metropolis that has prospered without developing the ethnic diversity that has become one of the defining characteristics of 'the city' across the globe.

4. The Streets

Once you have your city named, with the core of a population in place, whether attracted by ambition, greed or desperation, the next step in navigating a city is at the level of the individual street. However if cities actually depend on streets or not was the subject of a great deal of heated debate during the birth of architecture's modern movement at the beginning of the twentieth century. Le Corbusier was scornful of pavement cafés eating up space, and winding roads that, as he put it, reflected the random blind path of the donkey, and proposed what he maintained was a much healthier option of streets in the sky and massive apartment buildings in orthogonal ranks, rising out of parkland. In debased form it is a vision that has been realized in cities as different as Brasília and Marseilles, often with little success.

Streets, whatever Le Corbusier's view, are more than investments in infrastructure. They support the ability of a city's people to be able to move around their city in any way and at any time they choose. A clear set of marked street names reflects a democratic openness. It allows any stranger who is able to read to navigate a city while retaining their anonymity. This is not something that the autocrats who start some cities, and end up in control of others, are very enthusiastic about permitting. It makes them distrust cities in general, and streets in particular. In Imperial China, Beijing was built to be read as a diagram of heaven, with a layout that segregated the emperor from the elite, and the elite from the subservient, through a series of interlocking concentric courtyards. Mao's China controlled its proletariat in Beijing in similar fashion by creating a series of autonomous compounds for factories, which their occupants rarely left. And it prevented the publication of detailed maps of the city. In the early days of the Chinese opening to the West, foreign visitors who wanted to avoid the constraints of an official guide had no option but to acquire a copy of the map produced by the CIA through clandestine means.

The experience of a street is shaped by the relationship between pedestrians and vehicles. For much of the twentieth century, the urban fabric was being reconfigured for the car, with a severely negative impact on traditional street life. Critics of Western capitalism point to the privatization of public space and the way in which new cities allow for the movement of cars rather than pedestrians as anti-democratic. They militate against the kind of street life that encourages social interaction between strangers. Pedestrianization, which is often associated with the privatization of the public realm, can also suck life out of a public street by marooning it in the midst of the hard-to-cross ring roads created to cope with displaced traffic.

Once laid out, the effects of a street, whether they have a name or not, go on reverberating down the centuries. Decisions taken pragmatically by engineers, expediently by entrepreneurs or instinctively by pedestrians continue to shape everyday city life for centuries, even as the buildings that stand on those streets come and go.

It is the street that provides us with a place to share city life, to experience the culture of congestion. The connections and patterns of movement established by streets are what allow shops, houses, offices and institutions to coexist. Streets are the means by which cities grow and flourish, but also what can cause them to sicken and die if their vitality is threatened by street crime that frightens pedestrians away, or by rent rises that force out specialist shops. They are the product of a mix of architecture and economics, of vision and greed, infrastructure and fashion. Streets reflect the roots and the histories of cities. Both Oxford Street in London and the Via Condotti in Rome were once arteries of ancient Rome. Divanyolu, in Istanbul, takes the same route that the main street of Byzantium once did, laid out before the birth of Christ. The Champs-Élysée in Paris, which began as an extension to the gardens of the Tuileries in the seventeenth century, became the setting for France's monument to Napoleon's victories, the giant Arc de Triomphe. As a result, it was also the route of the German army's victory parade when they entered Paris in 1940.

Unter den Linden in Berlin, Chang'an Avenue in Beijing, and London's Downing Street have each become the backdrop for statecraft of very different kinds. From the middle of the eighteenth century, Unter den Linden was one of Berlin's successive attempts to establish the urban scenery of a capital city, straining to present itself at the head of the kingdom of Prussia, and then of the new German empire. In the 1950s, Chang'an Avenue, along with Tiananmen Square, was the biggest mark that Mao made on a city built to celebrate the power of the emperors. He had the old city walls, and many of their gates, demolished. Downing Street is still the personification of British understatement, a seat of government camouflaged as a domestic residence, in an apparently innocuous eighteenth-century city street.

In many cities, streets are transformed from generation to generation as they grow. Avenida Paulista in São Paulo was once a semi-rural residential boulevard lined by elaborate mansions. It is now thick with banks and the heart of South America's largest city with a population approaching 20 million. It is São Paolo's factories that produce the avionics for the country's burgeoning aircraft industry and make it possible for Brazil to launch satellites. And it is São Paolo's television studios that churn out the telenovelas that have a grip on the popular imagination of half the world. It has the biggest Japanese community in the world outside Japan. It has the largest fleet of privately owned helicopters in any city in the world. It also has a mayor who is able to ban outdoor street advertising overnight in a bid to beautify his city, a prison system permanently on the brink of insurrection, street children and police death squads. In this apparently formless sprawl, the Avenida provides one of the few instantly recognizable pieces of urban scenery.

Omotesandō in Tokyo, laid out before the Second World War, was once edged by the most progressive social-housing project in Japan. It is now the centre for fashion in the city, and is lined with trophy stores built for the biggest brands by the most expensive architects available.

Floral Street in London was once a route to a square of the city's most fashionable seventeenth-century houses in Covent Garden, with an Inigo Jones church in the piazza behind it. It was taken over by the vegetable market, which drove out the prosperous. When the present Royal Opera House was built in the nineteenth century, it turned its back on the market, and patrons arrived under the protection of a police station opposite its front entrance. When the market moved out in the 1970s, the area briefly turned into the heart of the counterculture while planners debated plans to drive new roads through the neighbourhood. When these plans were cancelled, and the market building was turned into a shopping mall, Floral Street went through an accelerated gentrification cycle. It went from fashionable to mass market in less than a decade, in a way that undermined its attractiveness to recreational shoppers, before a set of new owners did their best to transform it into an area of shops full of luxury goods.

Silbury Boulevard in Milton Keynes used a name that was calculated to inject a degree of other-worldliness into what appeared to be a materialist, car-dominated grid plan for a modern city. The shopping centre, which is its largest landmark, is aligned to allow the rising sun to shine directly along its central mall at the summer solstice.

The traditional street is now under threat from the cruder grain of mall-based consumerism, from web retailing and from the motor car. And yet there is a continuing hunger for its pedestrian scale, and its diversity. A hunger that is behind the proliferation of such elaborately fabricated evocations of pedestrian pavements as Main Street at Disneyland Paris in Marne-la-Vallée, South Las Vegas Boulevard in Las Vegas, Third Street Promenade in Santa Monica or Universal Studio's City Walk in Hollywood.

Brasília doesn't have pedestrian streets with pavements, a reflection of the prejudices of Lúcio Costa, the man who planned it, and his mentor Le Corbusier. Instead it has boulevards built for the needs of the car. Even worse than having little in the way of streets, it has no street corners, and therefore no chance for random encounters that come from one street meeting another, or for the potential of street-corner lounging that is a centuries-old practice of European cities, even if it is questionable how meaningful such interactions can be. Revealingly, an address in Brasília rarely includes a street name. It is based on a set of numerical and alphabetical codes that designate spaces on an invisible grid, defined by the monumental main avenue that runs east to west cutting the city in two. Every address is marked as either in the north or south wing on each side of the avenue. Within both wings there are designated single-use zones for banking, hotels and business, each with their own letter code. They need to be decoded in guidebooks for visitors. SHS, for example, would be *Setor Hoteleiro Sul*; SBN is *Setor Bancário Norte*. Each *setor* is made up of a number of *quadras*, groups of 10 or so buildings. In each *quadra* individual buildings are *conjunto* (*conj*) or *bloco* (*B* or *Bl*). Occupants in the block get a number. A full address would be something like SCS, Q 7, Bl A, loja 43, allowing you to find shop number 43 in building A in *quadra* 7 in the south commercial zone. It's a system that is a perfect reflection of Brasília's aspirations to be seen as the most modern, most up-to-date of cities, one which refused to be defined by traditional architecture or even conventional addresses, even at the cost of an apparent rationality making it incomprehensible to visitors.

5. Navigation

Names are not the only way to make sense of a city. Just as an architect should be able to find a way to indicate to visitors where to find the entrance to a hospital or a theatre, without having to resort to incorporating the word 'Entrance' over the front door, so there are techniques that planners and architects use to make cities legible. Often mistakenly, we are conditioned to interpret buildings that are elaborate and imposing as somehow more important than those that are simpler and more austere. We understand formal street layouts, of which symmetry is the most obvious characteristic, as reflecting spaces that aspire to civic qualities. Even when a city is laid out over many years, each step can be used to build on previous incarnations to make a city navigable; they define routes through them that make them intelligible without words.

Navigating cities takes more than names and maps. They are shaped and given form by their streets and roads, by their landmarks as well as their topography. Sometimes the landmarks are the unintended consequences of infrastructure. The Ministry of

Public Building and Works designed the Post Office Tower for over-the-horizon microwave transmissions. It also gave London its first structure that was taller than St Paul's. In its mid-century glass skin, like an office block turned into a needle, the tower became an unlikely signifier for London. It is different from but clearly part of the same family of communications masts that distinguish East Berlin and Shanghai. Tower Bridge was a technological solution to providing an uninterrupted river crossing for pedestrians at a high level even when the main bridge was opened to allow shipping to pass. London's double-decker buses have come to be essential parts of London's identity, as if they were a more pragmatic version of the Eiffel Tower built to mark the centenary of the French Revolution in 1889.

We are attracted to cities in part because they offer us the chance to find people and things that we did not know existed, and that we did not know that we wanted to find before we went there. A city offers chance social encounters, and places in which new ideas are being shaped. We need to have the opportunities to find them. In a business park, in which each building is crammed with graduate students writing algorithms, we will never encounter the students because they are insulated from the world outside by lawns kept watered by hissing irrigation systems, and defended from interlopers by gates guarded by swipe cards. Navigating a city is a bit like negotiating a way through a library. Randomly stacked shelves mean that their contents are lost to us, or reveal themselves only through random encounters, but some form of categorization gives us the chance to explore in a purposeful way.

A successful city is a place in which it is possible to feel a sense of shared community, but also a place in which it is entirely possible to flourish without feeling part of anything. That is the essence of a city, to choose from it what you need, and to politely ignore the rest.

The possibility of anonymity is one of the most important qualities that differentiates a city from a village. The city at its best allows for difference, and tolerance. To walk into a bar or a store, to rent a room or buy a book or log in to the web without having to account for who you are, or where you have come from, is a precious quality.

We navigate streets that have names, and roads that mostly have numbers, and now with the use of digital coordinates we are guided by satellite signals. Obviously street names can usefully describe topographies and indicate functional differentiation or orientation. Hill Street, Market Street and South Street would be examples. They also show the resonances and the depths of the historical layers in a city. The traces of the north Italian bankers who set up in London at the end of the Middle Ages are still faintly reflected in Lombard Street, the address that they left behind.

Street names are a declaration of political intent as well as a navigational tool. The American artist Susan Hiller's *The J. Street Project* documented the 303 streets across Germany that incorporated the word 'Juden' in their names before 1933 and explored their subsequent history. The Nazis removed every single street name with a Jewish reference. With the restoration of democracy in the West, the streets mostly went back to their original names; in some cases side by side with their Nazi-era versions to provide a historical record. In East Germany, there was another version of this policy. Some Jewish references were more acceptable than others. Karl Marx and early members of the Communist movement were fine, Prussian officers and businessmen less so. Is returning to a street name that once defined a ghetto a tribute to a murdered people or a memory of the discrimination against them? In some cases renaming can be a dangerous act of deliberate forgetting rather than a reversal of an injustice. With reunification, the cities of the former DDR lost their

Karl-Marx-Allee, along with their socialist realist memorials to Engels and Rosa Luxemburg. Some fought to preserve both: a sign not so much of their continuing belief in totalitarianism as a mark of their emotional commitment to retaining a sense of their own distinctive identity in the face of a more prosperous and more successful Western neighbour. Given the speed and frequency with which street signs have come down, getting around some Eastern European capital cities has become a challenge. Many Belgrade taxi drivers, for example, have lost track of the names of some of the city's major thoroughfares as it has gone from being the capital of Yugoslavia to the capital of Serbia. And what will happen to Union Street in Aberdeen, Perth and Glasgow if Scotland ever does vote 'Yes' in another independence referendum?

Financial calculation triggers name changes as readily as political upheaval. Manchester's Ancoats district was where Friedrich Engels began his inquiry into the condition of the English working classes and found them living in unendurable squalor. In the 1960s, the past was swept away by a wave of council-house building, and the area was renamed the Cardroom Estate. Its inhabitants had bathrooms, indoor lavatories, living rooms and kitchens that complied with the Parker Morris space standards that were the measure of the Welfare State at its most civilized. But such material improvements were not enough to allow a community to flourish and, when these houses too were demolished by a private house builder, they renamed the area New Islington in the hope that it would wash away the taints of both of the old names. Cardiff's Tiger Bay waterfront was recast as Cardiff Bay for similar reasons. Developers building housing for profit use a change of name to signal the departure of the poor and the imminent arrival of more affluent residents.

Street names are used to create a sense of identity and cohesion, and also of exclusion. America, pushed by the enthusiasm of its realtors for creating fashionable new districts from thin air, has developed a weakness for acronyms. It began harmlessly enough in Manhattan with SoHo, but has now worked its way through TriBeCa and NoLIta to the risible DUMBO, the latter creating somewhere out of a nowhere that was the segment of Brooklyn 'Down Under the Manhattan Bridge Overpass'.

British developers, however, have become obsessed with the idea of 'Quarters', As in the 'Merchants' Quarter', as that part of Bristol once known as Broadmead was briefly designated, until it was decided that this might be interpreted as honouring the activities in the slave trade of some of those merchants. It's a usage that can be traced back to the Prince of Wales's preferred architect, Léon Krier, and his pet project, the New Urbanism. It was used to suggest a commitment to mixed use and human-scale planning but now means little more than the word 'estate' once did. This, when first applied to British social housing, implied an optimistic utopia, as if the proletariat had acquired their own country seats, but it has now descended into signifying a dumping ground for social undesirables. In similar usage on Chicago's South Side, and other American cities, the housing authority projects were called 'Homes'.

Streets have the ability to become brands. Harley Street means medicine around the world, just as Savile Row means tailoring and Wall Street means finance, even if both the last two are losing their distinctive qualities. Rodeo Drive and Via della Spiga mean fashion and Basin Street means jazz and tourism. And none of them need the qualification of being attached to their specific cities. Brick Lane's street signs, now rendered in Bengali as well as English, can be seen both as a mark of respect to the Bangladeshi migrants who came to London in the 1970s, or as a piece of marketing-led branding as condescending as the pagoda roofs on the phone booths in San Francisco's Chinatown. The builders of London's great estates from the eighteenth century onwards were the land-owning families who treated property as a long-term investment, rather than the hit-and-run business that it has become. They used their own names for the streets that they built, or allowed to be built: Grosvenor, De Walden, Bedford, Sloane and the rest. It is a practice that could be understood as a more refined version of the tags left behind in aerosol spray by graffiti artists. And it can lead to some confusion. Just how many streets in London are there in close proximity in Belgravia with the word 'Cadogan' in their name? Others use place names derived from their country estates. The streets of Holland Park, for example, are sprinkled with places names from Somerset and Dorset. Equally confusing is the lack of consistency in numbering streets.

In an America caught between the ruthless logic of a numbered grid plan for so many of its cities and the nation-building impulse demonstrated by the ubiquitous stars and stripes that fly over so many suburban lawns, there is a strictly limited range of street names used over and over again. According to the US Census, the most common street name in America is a number: Second Street. This is closely followed by a selection of trees: Elm, Pine, Oak, then Park, and a few dead presidents all of which you will find in almost every US city. In Mexico City, there are whole sequences of streets named for philosophers, from Descartes to Kant, which give way to other sequences of writers, presidents, doctors and artists. They border on streets named for European nation states. It is a system that suggests rapid urbanization with large numbers of streets to name in a short period of time. To find yourself in a street named for Pasteur, next to one named after Beneš, the first president of Czechoslovakia, is a reminder that Mexico is also a united states, a nation formed by migration from all over the world. This is not something that you will find in a British city, where Boer War battlefields are more likely inspirations for street names.

Like the random accidents of history that permanently imprint themselves as the invisible structure of daily life, of which the QWERTY keyboard is perhaps the most all-pervasive, we use chance phenomena to navigate and make sense of the city. London is still defined by the postal districts that the Victorians first devised in 1856 and implemented in 1857–8 to help simplify the task of delivering mail. They categorized the city in the clusters of letters and numbers that have metamorphosed into a kind of social register, separating the deprived from the suburban and the smart from the underclass. SW1 and SW3 spell out varying degrees of affluence. But if you live in NW10, you know that you will be at least within hearing distance of gun crime and gang wars.

It's a message that is underscored by the street signs themselves, with each borough using its own typography and graphic language. Westminster has white enamel signs with an elegant modernist font. In Hampstead, each letter is in a bold serif, rendered on glazed ceramic tile. In a small way it is as much of a place-maker as a red bus or a London taxi. There are cases of American zip codes playing a similar social role, although since they are not always used on street signs they are not quite so present in the urban landscape. But New York certainly looks a different place now that it has taken down 250,000 street signs all in capitals Highway Gothic and replaced them with new signs in upper- and lower-case letters in the new Clearview font, at the insistence of the Federal Government in the belief that it is more legible, and therefore safer.

There are niceties of detail to be observed in the way in which cities represent themselves. A fine-grained European city can rely on elegant typographic signs pinned to street corners. It is not the same in Korea after its turbocharged emergence from poverty as the largest single recipient of US foreign aid, to First World affluence in the course of a single lifetime. Korea has created what to European eyes look like intimidatingly regimented cities, with tens of thousands of people living in identical parallel high-rise slabs, each block identified by its own number, rendered four floors high. Tokyo has few street names, bar the boulevards such as Meiji Dori that were laid out when the city was being Westernized. Instead it has a ward system in which each address has three numbers. Like Brasília it numbers ward, block and building, which are not consecutive but refer to the sequence in which individual houses were built, and their distance from a local landmark.

It is more than an eccentricity in descriptive forms: Japan's cities – with the exception of Kyoto, which has a grid – are organized, understood and navigated in ways that are different from Western cities. Or at least they were until the universal availability of GPS. Navigating Tokyo used to depend on sketch maps, diagrams based on local landmarks, and subway stations, confirmed by phone calls en route. You could find such informal drawings on the back of business cards, or sent by fax at the start of a taxi ride. Today a moving three-dimensional map on the dashboard does the job. These technologies have already made traditional taxi licences redundant around the world. By the beginning of the next decade, self-driving vehicles will do the same for Uber's drivers. At the same time, by combining GPS calibration with the data that Transport for London has on precisely where every one of its buses, tube and overground trains is on its network at any given moment, London and its geography have been made much easier to understand, even for that minority of its inhabitants who were born and grew up in the city. The route-numbering system for its buses inherited from Victorian horse-drawn omnibuses is so obscure that nobody, even the Transport for London administration, understands its logic or remembers where more than a few of its routes will take them. The Citymapper app will tell you exactly which combination of routes to take to achieve your destination, and give you accurate timings to tell you when you will get there. It is a technology that is dramatically changing behaviours and transport usage; a phenomenon, of course, that is immediately mapped in the data that the system is based on. If more people use a route on the basis of the data that they get from their smartphone, bus frequencies can adjust to meet the demand. The idea of changing bus routes on a journey would once have seemed impossibly risky. Now Citymapper makes it a plausible option, encouraging users to take buses more often, and to take routes that they would never previously have known existed.

Technology is quickly superseding the old ways that we used to make sense of cities; but the subway map pioneered by London Transport still survives. Harry Beck's diagram for London has been much imitated and much interpreted. Beck was an electrical engineer who based his interpretation of the system on the graphic vocabulary of a circuit diagram, and who also had the insight to supplement it with a representation of the Thames as an orientating device. Design historians who are susceptible to conspiracy theories have speculated that the foreshortening of scale to the end of the line was deliberately designed to make the new residential developments being built in the 1930s, at these outer limits, appear more central and so more attractive to house buyers than they really were. In fact spacing stops equally across the whole system makes the centre where they are clustered closest together more legible.

Beck was no graphic designer, but he created one of the world's most potent graphic symbols for a city. His more stylish rival in the field was Massimo Vignelli who, working with his partner Bob Noorda, created a short-lived equivalent of the London map for the New York City Transit Authority in the 1970s. With its citrus-fruit-salad colours and its bold typography, Vignelli's work on New York's subway redefined modern Manhattan in the 1970s. When the city was at its lowest ebb, threatened by bankruptcy and a violent crime wave, the signage and the maps were optimistic alternatives in the midst of all the decay; a sign of better times to come that ran throughout the decrepit system of the 1970s. It was called a map but what Vignelli and his collaborators actually produced was a diagram. It is an important distinction. The diagram suggested that Central Park was wider and shorter than it actually is. But that wasn't the point. Vignelli wanted to help travellers make sense of a complex system, and to work out where to change trains, not use the diagram to navigate the streets above the tracks. The Transit Authority didn't see it that way, and withdrew Vignelli's work, to replace it with a less confident-looking hybrid.

Streets have names. Roads that have been designed for cars rather than pedestrians mostly have numbers. What we have yet to understand is whether the road is an adequate replacement for the street. The world fell in love with the car and the freedom that it seemed to offer. We spent 50 years reshaping all our cities to accommodate it. Despite a lingering passion for the charms of the car we have been consumed by remorse, but only when it was too late to go back to the old world.

Adapting cities for cars came later than is sometimes assumed. Los Angeles is the most celebrated example of a city defined by its roads. But its first period of explosive growth was actually the product of its streetcars. They ran along what were called boulevards. It was only later in the 1940s when the freeway system got going, and the city really started to sprawl, that the boulevards with names were eclipsed by freeways with numbers, which now define much urban geography. The M25, or London Orbital, is the distinctive British contribution to motorway building. It may owe something to Washington's Beltway, or the Périphérique in Paris, but it's the largest of its kind in Europe, longer even than Moscow's third ring, though not as big as Beijing's sixth, and the only one designed for right-hand-drive cars.

The M25 is the product of an endlessly long-drawn-out planning process. It took 15 years to finish the 118 miles of motorway which serves to define the shape and the identity of London. The M25 is as important a London address as Oxford Street or the King's Road.

The digital revolution has made new kinds of urban space, both physical and virtual, possible. Social media is an alternative to public meetings for citizens, and to café conspiracies for terrorists. It allows people to meet who would never have found each other in the traditional urban world. We navigate with the coordinates of GPS systems. We never need miss a train connection, or wait at a bus stop in the rain, or find ourselves lost in unfamiliar streets. But digital communication is also threatening to turn the city back into a village in which Google's search engines mean that there are no more strangers. The city's anonymity and its privacy are under threat as never before from Google's cameras, Apple's location-based services and pervasive security.

The archetypal city of the third Industrial Revolution could be taken to mean a city continually under scrutiny, policed by number-plate-recognition systems, kept moving by Uber, and crowd monitoring on the metro. The uses that we make of the iPhone and the cash machine leave an indelible trail. This is turning the city into a compound in which every action is known; every form of behaviour can be predicted; every dissident tracked and monitored.

One definition of the traditional city is an identifiable street name and number: the greater their density, the more like a city the place is. But for much of the world these are few and far between. Digital technology is now being applied to define the estimated four billion inhabitants of Earth without an address. OkHi offers a web address with an attached image of the front door; what3words is more ambitious: every three-metre grid square in the world has been assigned an identifier in three recognizable words, available in a choice of languages.

If digital communication is undermining the physical city, the internet may also offer a possible alternative form of urbanism. Like all authentic cities, this digital city has both its light and its dark side. Crime and vice hover at the edges of virtual public space that also encompasses the free public library with unlimited information that is Wikipedia. Twitter is the twenty-first-century equivalent of the lavatory wall, a place for the scurrilous and the psychopathic to leave their mark, and also, if we are generous, an electronic version of the posters on Beijing's Democracy Wall at the end of the Mao years. The result is a polyglot mix of the inspirational and the banal, the marketplace and the propaganda machine, the vicious and the benign.

The digital world impacts on cities at every level: from street navigation to social geography, from an app to Airbnb, which can transform a residential street into a hotel district, and turn a home into a revenue-generating asset shared by strangers.

A city is defined at a range of different scales, and it remains to be seen what cities will form at the level of the Cloud, or how they will diminish in the physical realm. For now, it is still true that the identity of the city, as a whole, starts with its name. It is reflected in the way in which its people speak, the ways in which they navigate the city. It is there in the details of civic life, and in the monuments that define its physical form as well as its history. These are the elements that build up over time to create the city's personality and its identifying marks. Once formed, they are not easily erased or forgotten. They form the starting points and references for everything that follows. But they can be changed or undermined. They contain the traces of a city's past and the basis for its evolution.

Chapter Three

How to Change a City

Cabot Place, on the Isle of Dogs, London E14, is in the borough of Tower Hamlets, but not of it. It is an address that conveys the explosive transformation of a city with no more than a cryptic whisper. Cabot Place is a shopping mall rather than a conventional street; a glossy travertine-lined bubble at the foot of what was, very briefly, the tallest office tower in Europe. It sits at the centre of Canary Wharf, on top of what was once the heart of Britain's busiest dock complex.

John Cabot, otherwise known as Giovanni Caboto, was a fifteenth-century Italian explorer probably born in Genoa. Under contract to Henry VII, the English king, Cabot set off to find a route sailing north and west to Asia in 1497. He never managed it but he did get as far as Newfoundland, which was to become the first building block of Britain's empire and eventually form part of Canada.

There are Cabot Streets throughout Canada, and a Cabot Circus in Bristol, but in London it is a much rarer street name. Cabot Place is inside the Canary Wharf complex. It is now owned by a partnership between the state of Qatar and the Brookfield development company.

Cabot did not begin his voyage of discovery from London. When he left England he saved a week's sailing time in his journey north-west by starting from Bristol. Ships docking in London in those days tied up at Billingsgate and the other wharves upstream. At the end of the fifteenth century, the Isle of Dogs was remote marshland.

The attempt to link Cabot's name to the Canary Wharf development, in a city with which he had no personal connection, is an attempt to inject some sort of historical resonance into the fabric of a new slice of the city. Cabot was involved with trade and shipping, as Canary Wharf once had been. The new Canary Wharf was being positioned as a place for merchant adventurers with the ambition to match that of Cabot. It was also hinting at a connection with Canada.

Canary Wharf, with a working population of at least 110,000 at the last count – a third of the population of the borough as a whole – and with global clout as a financial centre, is as big as many towns but isn't yet 30 years old. In its difficult early days it struggled to attract occupants. Like many new cities it needed a backstory to get it started.

The references to Cabot in Canary Wharf are a reflection of the origins of the Reichmann family, who made their fortune in property in Toronto in the 1960s. It suggests their wish to leave their mark, in the most discreet way, on this project by paying tribute to the country in which they finally settled, having fled Vienna in the early 1930s.

That such attempts to use names to evoke historic or political associations can be done more heavy-handedly was demonstrated by the unrealized project to the east of Hay's Wharf, now the site of London's new City Hall, initiated by the government of Kuwait. The plan had been to build a sequence of office blocks each named for one of a procession of Conservative prime ministers, starting with Lord North, and working its way up to Margaret Thatcher.

In its efforts to establish its historical provenance, Canary Wharf has followed the example of many newly founded cities. In Brasília the tomb of Juscelino Kubitschek contains the surveying instruments used to set out the city, and has the character of a pharaonic memorial. It is the place that new visitors or younger residents are taken to see the official story of the foundation of the city. There are fanciful alternative accounts of the city's origins not represented here. At the airport obscure cult members gather to hand out maps that suggest Brasília was originally laid out according to principles inspired by ancient Egyptian astronauts.

A more traditional foundation myth is on display in the public spaces of Siena in Italy, which are adorned by representations of Romulus and Remus cast in bronze. Siena's myth is that the city was established after Romulus murdered his brother. His two nephews fled from Rome, bringing the statue of the wolf suckling two infants with them.

Canary Wharf was once at the heart of the West India Docks, a place that fuelled and fed London. The borough of Tower Hamlets has housed London's port for centuries, though it was only at the very start of the nineteenth century that Britain's burgeoning capitalist class began to invest in the infrastructure needed to load and unload the ships that were growing larger and more numerous. In the years leading up to the Napoleonic Wars, English and Scottish engineers created the basins in which ships could be insulated from the tidal river. Their precious cargoes were protected from theft by a 20-foot-high brick wall that surrounded the entire site. The docks were once lined by travelling cranes, and cluttered with shipping from around the world. The banana boats, passenger ships and tramp steamers had all vanished by 1980, leaving emptiness and mirror smooth basins, disturbed only occasionally by the arc of a bird taking flight.

Now, in the new malls that form a base for the office towers, there are the usual mid-market chain restaurants. There are enough bankers in the area to keep a Corney & Barrow wine merchant in business, a Tiffany outlet for them to buy their cufflinks at lunchtime, and a Paul Smith shop to let them change their shirts. Five levels down in the Norman Foster-designed station is the Jubilee Line tube that can deliver the bankers to their homes in the stucco-fronted palaces of Holland Park in less than 30 minutes when they do not have the patience to do it in a chauffeured Mercedes.

At ground level Canary Wharf began as a film-set version of a central London square. The line of taxis at a granite kerb on the

Chapter Three

It took three decades (as shown by the images on these pages, which were taken thirty years apart), to turn London's derelict docklands into one of the world's most powerful financial centres. The transformation was the result of a sequence of unintended consequences. The shipping container abolished upstream docks around the world. The attempt to regenerate the docks was never expected to turn wharves into skyscrapers. But the inducements on offer to build industrial sheds were also available for banks and created an unexpected, unplanned financial centre – Canary Wharf – shown opposite.

pavement outside Morgan Stanley's offices looks authentic enough as the drivers wait for the director to call 'Action'. But Morgan Stanley itself, designed at the height of the postmodern boom by the American architects SOM in the manner of Louis Sullivan's nineteenth-century Carson Pirie Scott & Co. department store in Chicago, looks as if it has lurched in from another movie. There are pedestrians here, but very few other forms of traffic except for the taxis. Private cars are corralled in the car park two levels down.

What looks like a slice of London when seen through half-closed eyes, and which appears to have the diversity and the accidental qualities of what you might call a free-range city, is in fact the result of clearly preprogrammed decisions. It may look like part of a city but every inch of the 97 acres of Canary Wharf – except for the underground stations and a few fragments of the riverfront – is private property. Its owners demand that anybody who wants to take photographs on their land apply and pay for a permit in advance. The rights that come with ownership allow them to prevent a political demonstration, stop strikers picketing and bar charities from collecting.

But there are signs now that the development has taken on a life of its own. On the 35th floor of the first tower, the Canary Wharf Company maintains half a floor of models, like the Egyptian map room in the *Raiders of the Lost Ark*. It shows the original development, in models that represent completed buildings, and then, clustered around them are the new projects that are now beginning. They are lifted up on a baseboard at waist height, and are tall enough to intimidate visitors.

Further models of the intricate plans at ground and basement levels show the evolution of the project. What were once floors of car parking have been made redundant as the mass transit links with the rest of London have strengthened. Some of the cars have gone to make way for more shopping floors.

The most striking new model is of an apartment tower designed by Herzog & de Meuron, architects of the Beijing Olympic Stadium. The addition of homes to Canary Wharf is a reflection of the massive returns on residential property in London that can make it more profitable than building offices. But it is also a sign that the development is mutating in ways that the Reichmann brothers could never have predicted. It is, in fact, beginning to outgrow the ability of any single developer to control it. It has escaped from its compound and is spreading into the city beyond its boundaries with its own version of urbanism like an invasive species.

Outside this bubble-within-a-bubble is Tower Hamlets: a different universe in which the borough's first directly elected mayor was removed from office after having been shown to be stuffing ballot boxes and bribing his electorate.

A mile north of Canary Wharf, Chrisp Street Market is more typical of Tower Hamlets. The market is the product of Welfare State planners in the 1950s attempting to inject new life into the East End. It was meant to be a modern version of a souk. Its architects tried to create a sense of energy by piling apartments on top of shops and making a densely packed pedestrian complex, with bridges, terraces and roof gardens. It set a pattern for social housing that was repeated all over Britain in the 1970s. And it led, mostly, to abandoned parades of shops, with a few fortified survivors, concrete stalactites dripping from the overhead walkways and alleys cluttered by abandoned shopping trolleys. Chrisp Street is an exception. As Somalis, Kosovans, Bangladeshis and Kurds began to move to London, it became a real market rather than an artificial one fabricated by architects who had been to Marrakech on their student travels.

Once Canary Wharf had taken shape, the architect David Adjaye deftly slipped a new library building into this context. It takes the form of a multicoloured ribbon of glass built on an

In Shanghai, the mayor built a public showcase (above) to celebrate his vision of what the city would one day become. Beijing followed suit a few years later with its equally elaborate model (opposite).

abandoned roof garden on top of a single-storey mall of shops. From Canary Wharf the market is invisible. But looking south from Chrisp Street, the skyscrapers of Canary Wharf seem almost close enough to reach out and touch. There are some bankers and tax lawyers who work in Canary Wharf who come from the same places as the refugees, asylum seekers and migrants searching for a better life who live in Poplar and who use the market. But the only points of contact between these two very different Londons are the cleaners who live in Poplar and enter Canary Wharf's towers during the small hours to tidy offices and empty rubbish bins for the minimum wage.

Canary Wharf is a place that has little space for memories, even those of the IRA bombing campaign that once targeted its towers. Two lives were lost and 100 people were injured, but there is nothing to remind us of the death and trauma. Tenants come and go without leaving the faintest trace. When the *Daily Telegraph* moved out of Fleet Street, it left behind the swaggering art deco monument a previous proprietor had built for the paper. It is a listed landmark now, protected from demolition with all the force of law. The paper spent a decade in Canary Wharf but every trace of its time there has evaporated. The *Telegraph* left its name in Fleet Street in cut stone and cast bronze. But when the removal men had taken out the last filing cabinet and the last office chair from Canary Wharf, the new tenants dismantled the *Telegraph*'s temporary partitions, unscrewed their Perspex signs in the lift lobby and left nothing.

In the midst of the Prouvé chairs in the Canary Wharf branch of the Ask pizzeria chain and the peri-peri chicken in Nando's, there is at least one suggestion of time passing and of individual lives being allowed to make a mark. The consumer sheen of Cabot Place is interrupted by a bronze relief made by the artist Gerald Laing that was unveiled by Eddie George, the Governor of the Bank of England at the time. Laing, sometimes described as a pop artist, also had a line in conventional representational sculpture, of which the Cabot Place sculpture is an example. Below a somewhat stilted depiction of Michael von Clemm's profile, a man who died unexpectedly young of a brain tumour at the age of 62, are the words 'Investment banker and pioneer of the Euromarkets whose vision helped to create this financial centre'. Michael von Clemm was a brilliant, if somewhat abrasive, American-born banker, with a parallel career as an anthropologist at Harvard and Oxford.

Cities are shaped either by those who have a vision of what they might be, or by those who see an opportunity. Von Clemm certainly saw a financial opportunity on the Isle of Dogs. His interest in currency trading began from what he saw of local barter systems while undertaking research as an anthropologist in Tanzania. That insight would eventually lead to the creation of the Eurobond market in which von Clemm played an important part. Von Clemm ran Credit Suisse First Boston. He invested in the Roux brothers and their three-star Michelin restaurant that did a lot to change the eating habits of Britain's affluent classes. It was perhaps his ability to analyse how societies worked and use that analysis in the context of finance that gave him the insight to see what Canary Wharf could become. And it was that insight which triggered the process that transformed London's endless acres of derelict dockland into what has become, after the Square Mile of the City of London, Europe's largest financial centre.

There was another American who had no known vision of the future of cities but who should also be credited for his unwitting contribution to the making of Canary Wharf. On 5 October 1957, one of Malcolm McLean's ships set sail from Newark to Miami, its hold stacked with a cargo of steel boxes 40 feet long, 8 feet wide and 8 feet 6 inches high. The shipping container, a very basic piece of low technology, developed by the Fruehauf

Trailer Company to McLean's specifications, would quickly have the impact of a neutron bomb on every upstream port city in the world. In the course of two decades, McLean's invention wiped out every enclosed dock, from Tower Bridge to Silvertown and North Woolwich, in favour of container terminals. It took a whole way of life with it and created a void in London's fabric that von Clemm's insight would eventually fill. It might also be argued that the Canary Wharf development is what set off an explosive change in the rest of London's physical character.

In February 1985, in the midst of Margaret Thatcher's second government, when Britain was still in the grip of an economic trauma, von Clemm was driven down for lunch at Canary Wharf with Michel Roux. They were looking for somewhere to build a 5,000-square-foot warehouse to prepare and store chilled food. This was a moment when the docks, which once employed 25,000 people directly, and on whose prosperity another 75,000 jobs depended, had been all but abandoned. The Greater London Council had been so pessimistic about the likelihood of bringing it back to life that they debated tearing down the dock walls and turning all the land inside them into a giant park.

Thatcher abolished the GLC before it had the chance to put that, or any other idea for the future of the docks, into practice. To make sure there was no chance that the administration she detested would ever return, the florid Edwardian baroque County Hall building across the Thames from the Palace of Westminster, in which councillors had deliberated since 1922, was sold off to a Japanese owner in 1990 and turned into a curiously unappetizing mix of hotel, Chinese restaurant, art gallery and aquarium. All cultural ambition came to an abrupt end 10 years later when Charles Saatchi moved his collection out of the old Members' Terrace and the London Dungeon arrived.

The end of London's County Hall as a landmark of civic democracy was just one aspect of a wider struggle between an unusually ideological Conservative government and a Britain in which many of the biggest cities were run by left-wing local politicians. The conflict came to a head in the riots of 1981, when some of the most deprived neighbourhoods of London, Manchester and Liverpool burned. The uprising was an outburst from a young generation that had no connection with conventional politics, but it had a dramatic impact on the government. The shock of seeing police lines breached, night after night, Molotov cocktails flying, and the serious damage done to the country's reputation for stability, gave the Prime Minister pause and persuaded her to put her combative environment minister, Michael Heseltine, in charge of reviving Britain's cities. He established a development corporation for the docks, modelled on the organizations that had built the Welfare State's new towns in the 1950s and 1960s. The conventional rules of local government planning were suspended within the London Docklands Development Corporation's boundaries – north and south of the Thames. An enterprise zone was created in selected areas of the LDDC, an idea credited to the planning academic Peter Hall. Within the zone, planning regulations were simplified and a range of financial incentives introduced to encourage anyone prepared to set up a business in the docks. The offer included a 100 per cent tax write-off on the capital cost of building, and a 10-year tax holiday.

The LDDC was led by Reg Ward, a man who approached his task with few preconceptions. With truly spectacular pragmatism, he claimed not to have a detailed master plan, but was ready to spend his budget on step-by-step decisions that, as he put it, might become a coherent plan only in retrospect. He was, however, determined not to fill in the docks with concrete, as would very likely have been done if the project had started a decade earlier. The plan then would have been to make the area as normal as possible, to strip it of any distinguishing characteristics. It was what almost happened to the Albert Dock in Liverpool in the 1970s. Keeping the water made dockland distinctive; it allowed Ward to mount a billboard campaign that boasted of the new docklands: 'It will look like Venice, but work like New York'. This was not a message calculated to be conciliatory to the Labour politicians who had run the Greater London Council. Tony Banks, chairman of the arts and recreation committee, had set the tone for the last administration by insisting that the GLC-run Festival Hall shut down its champagne bar, a catering facility that he judged too elitist for the tastes of his proletarian electorate.

Within the limits of the resources that he had, Ward did his best to make the docks easier to get to. The LDDC invested in the Docklands Light Railway, a toy-like train of limited capacity that was cheaper and quicker to build than a high-capacity underground line (which would have been more useful). It began running somewhat fitfully in 1987. Ward also persuaded the Mowlem construction company to build a short take-off and landing runway for a new airport in the midst of the Royal Docks. In the early days landing there felt more like stunt flying than conventional air travel. Only specially trained pilots in certified aircraft were allowed to attempt one of the steepest descents in Europe. Beyond transport, Ward's architectural vision for the docks was limited. The LDDC hoped for a world of crinkly tin sheds with roll-up shutters to accommodate light-industrial jobs, perhaps with some housing, a mix not so different from what Ward had achieved in his earlier career as chief executive of Irvine New Town in Scotland. When a wine-distributing business and a TV production company took on Shed 31, a concrete slab on Canary Wharf where the boats bringing tomatoes from the Canary Islands had once tied up, the development corporation celebrated. Then von Clemm turned up with Michel Roux. The banker saw the chance of doing something rather different from worthy British new towns like Harlow. He had an idea for building what he took to be a city. The incentives on offer to new businesses to build in dockland could just as much be used to save tax bills on establishing offices for financiers as to help set up factories. What was turning into a suburban business park could still become a financial centre.

What eventually happened to Canary Wharf was planning as the result of unintended consequences. It was a version of London triggered by an insight that fully justifies von Clemm's memorial in Cabot Place. Credit Suisse's UK headquarters are in a 14-storey block at One Cabot Square, designed by Ieoh Ming Pei's one-time partner Harry Cobb, but von Clemm himself did not build Canary Wharf. He asked G. Ware Travelstead, the bank's flamboyant property adviser, who had trained as an architect, to take it on. Von Clemm thought Canary Wharf could be a place to put CSFB's back-office team. Travelstead wanted to move all of the bank's London operations there, taking the other international banks that had recently come to London with them. They had been attracted to Britain by the deregulation of banking and finance initiated by Margaret Thatcher, but were frustrated at the lack of what they believed would be appropriate space in the capital's traditional financial centre, the City of London. In the early 1980s, the city planners had adopted a policy that ruled out high-rises in the Square Mile, demanded the retention of existing façades for redevelopment projects and restricted the amount of new floor space. In response to one proposal for the design of a new office building in the City, Richard Rogers was handed a photocopy of an image of the Ca' d'Oro, a nineteenth-century Glaswegian office building based on a Venetian original, and it was suggested to him that it should form the model for a revised application. This was not the way that American bankers were used to being treated:

Travelstead came back to London six months later with a set of plans drawn up by Kohn Pedersen Fox, a firm that was establishing itself with a string of commercial towers that deliberately set out to differentiate themselves from the glass and steel formula adopted by a previous generation. Applied ornament and stone façades, albeit just a few inches thick, were essential parts of their repertoire. Arthur May, KPF's design partner, relied on a book on Hawksmoor's churches and their steeples that he kept at his drawing board for reference. He produced a master plan that would have seen a sequence of postmodern towers laid out in a symmetrical pattern on either side of a monumental central axis filling the whole of the dock zone of the Isle of Dogs. By this time, Limehouse Studios had already opened for business in a converted shed right in the middle of what KPF envisioned as the lift lobby for one of the central towers of the Manhattan-on-Thames that they had planned. It was clear that the Americans were determined to knock it down and start all over again.

It would be at least two years before the Dockland Light Railway (DLR) started running, and even when it did it was inconceivable that it could handle the 46,000 office workers Canary Wharf's first stage would accommodate. The proposals were greeted with scepticism: this was a project on a scale, and of a style, that the consciously conservative, dowdy and down-at-heel London of the mid-1980s simply did not go in for. Nevertheless, the LDDC were impressed. Letters of intent were signed, a foundation-stone-laying ceremony was staged. Exhibitions were sponsored, ministers were lobbied, and an elegant logo was drawn up for the development company established to do the job. But Travelstead simply did not have the track record to raise the £1 billion he needed to start building. And when von Clemm left Credit Suisse for Merrill Lynch in 1986, Travelstead's project foundered.

By this time the idea of a new financial district was out in the open. Sir Christopher Benson, chairman of the LDDC and himself a property developer, did not want to see it stall so he called Paul Reichmann, founder of Olympia & York, that, at the time, was one of the world's largest and most ambitious property companies, a conglomerate worth $20 billion at its height. Reichmann and his brothers had already built two massive office complexes: First Canadian Place in Toronto, and Battery Park City in New York. They had once owned a subsidiary in the UK, but sold it a few years earlier, claiming that the political climate was too unsympathetic for their business. Benson, with the help of an encouraging call from the Prime Minister, in which she suggested that the government would provide practical support by renting space in the development, managed to persuade the Reichmanns to take another look at London.

Many property companies work all over the world now. Olympia & York was one of the first to make global development into an essential business strategy. Paul Reichmann believed that spreading risk around the globe was a way to insure his company against local downturns and the boom-and-bust nature of the development business. The property cycle might be down in Europe and Asia simultaneously, but was unlikely also to be suffering in America at the same time. It was a perspective that made them look at Canary Wharf in global terms.

At the start of the 1980s, Tokyo had 400 million square feet of prime office space. New York had 300 million and London just 160 million. Looked at like that, paying £190 million for a 71 acre slice of London on which they could build perhaps six million square feet for £2 billion plus another £900 million as a contribution to the cost of extending the tube line out to the docks, seemed like a sound investment. In the long run they turned out to be right. By 2015, London's West End had the highest office rents in the world, and had done so for the previous three years running, ahead of Hong Kong, twice the price of Moscow and Beijing, and almost four times the cost of renting the most expensive building in Milan. Canary Wharf is not the same as the West End of London, but it had become valuable enough for a controlling stake to change hands for £2.6 billion when Qatar and the Brookfield company bought the entire estate in 2015.

The Reichmanns' Olympia & York was a company that liked to recruit talent from the other side of the negotiating table that it met in the course of doing business. The local government planners who approved their development applications ended up working for them, and were able subsequently to smooth their path in future projects. The brothers brought a whole team of people from Canada with them to explore the Canary Wharf prospect. Ron Soskolne, who had been a city planner, ran the detailed design of Canary Wharf, and George Iacobescu, a Romanian-born civil engineer who had fled to Canada from the Communists, built it and later took charge of the development company when the Reichmanns lost control.

Iacobescu still tells the story of coming to London at the start of the project. After he got to his hotel, he set out to walk to Canary Wharf so that he could get a sense of just how far this mooted new financial centre really was from the Bank of England, which, in the days before the Big Bang financial deregulation of 1986, when transactions were carried by messenger, insisted on keeping its charges close by. The route would have taken him along Cornhill and Leadenhall, past what was then the London Metal Exchange, down to Crosswall, past what were then run-down art deco buildings on the Minories, around the Tower of London, after which the landscape turned bleak. Further east Iacobescu skirted Cable Street, still the embodiment of the old East End, where Oswald Mosley's Blackshirts were turned back by a massive antifascist protest in 1936. He went past Limehouse Basin – built in the early nineteenth century as the interchange between the half-derelict canal network that circled London and the Thames – then along Narrow Street, which by this time already had a few warehouses that had been converted into lofts, and then finally to Canary Wharf. It took him more than an hour.

It was a chastening experience, one that made him understand just how massive was the task that faced his employers. The

World Financial Center at Battery Park City, the development that Olympia & York made into New York's third financial district, was the model, as the Reichmanns saw it, for Canary Wharf. In a crowded city with a tangled street plan that made it difficult to build giant open-plan dealing rooms, they believed they could find plenty of takers for unconstricted space close by. But Battery Park is just 15 minutes' walk from Wall Street. Canary Wharf, at more than four miles from the Bank of England, still looked and felt a world away. Travelstead's plan for Canary Wharf involved building a cluster of high-rises as its centrepiece. The Reichmanns scrapped that as uneconomic and started again, substituting a single central skyscraper, framed by two squares formed by groups of lower blocks sitting on top of a mall, with 6,500 parking places below ground.

It had to be all or nothing: as Iacobescu's pilgrimage from the Square Mile had taught him, the development would work only if it was big enough to achieve the critical mass that would make it look like a plausible financial centre right from the start. New occupants had to be made to feel they were in the midst of something as soon as they arrived. César Pelli, who had worked on Battery Park City, designed the first tower, with its aluminium skin and its pyramid top, to be Europe's tallest. 'Why,' the Prince of Wales asked when he was shown a model of the new development, 'does it have to be so tall?' Iacobescu could have told him the obvious: that it was intended to be a signpost, pointing to the site like a giant finger, visible from across London so that he could have followed it on his walk from the Bank of England. 'Step this way,' it was beckoning, in an attempt after five centuries to reverse London's headlong flight westward. Even the most sophisticated of twentieth-century developments need the most basic of things: a sign to tell us where to find them.

The Reichmanns staged an elaborate ceremony to mark their start on site. A fleet of launches, equipped with banks of the outsize mobile phones of the period, conveyed the press down the Thames to the site. The three brothers, observant Jews sombrely dressed in black and wearing skullcaps, welcomed the Prime Minister, Margaret Thatcher, to the ceremony.

Not everybody shared her enthusiasm. For the surrounding Labour-controlled boroughs, this vision of the docks as a centre for global finance was a betrayal, one that had nothing to offer them. Where were the new factories, the new schools, the libraries and the health centres? Equally hostile, though less vocal, and much more lethal in its covert objections, was the City of London. As soon as it became clear that Canary Wharf was going to stand a chance of succeeding as an office development capable of attracting prime financial industry tenants, the City reversed its existing policies and did what it could to undermine that success.

The City of London plan of 1985 was designed to preserve the character of the City as it was by introducing a ban on large-scale development, restricting changes of use and discouraging alterations to the existing street pattern. Even before the Reichmanns started building Canary Wharf, the City's strategy had come under heavy criticism from those who wanted to see more development not less. The Thatcherite think tank, the Centre for Policy Studies, argued violently against the City's plan and the attitudes behind it. They saw it as representing a straitjacket that threatened the very survival of the City, which, they argued, was Britain's most precious financial asset. 'New organizations are not going to put up with refurbished buildings lurking behind Victorian façades. The philosophy behind the plan unfortunately illustrates the national malaise of looking at the past and not the future which is the root of Britain's economic decline. The plan is based on superficial analysis and outdated ideas.' It seemed that they were right. When the old Billingsgate Fish Market on the Thames – just below the Monument marking the spot where the Great Fire of London that wiped out most of the City had started in 1666 – was converted into a vast dealing room, nobody moved in. Canary Wharf had become more attractive as an option.

The City's chief architect, Stuart Murphy, the man behind the City's plan, resigned. And so the unintended consequences of the shipping container that cleared the way for the accidental transformation of Canary Wharf into a financial centre triggered another accidental transformation: the conversion of the skyline of the City of London into what eventually became a European version of Shanghai or Dubai. Murphy was replaced in 1986 by Peter Rees, a planner who presided over the skyscraperization of London with what looked like self-regarding glee. Instead of insisting on keeping existing façades and modest footprints, and preventing high-rise development, the City granted a flood of planning permissions on its own territory, allowing developers to do almost exactly what they liked.

Along with a general downturn in Britain's economic outlook, it was enough to do serious damage to the Reichmanns' plans. Canary Wharf now struggled to find tenants. They were reduced to filling the first, and tallest, tower designed by César Pelli with journalists. (Coincidentally, this was the time that newspapers were able to introduce the new technology that could do without the need for a physical connection between newsroom and printing hall.) Fleet Street, which had seen the newspapers cluster together for a century, became redundant and central London's last remaining heavy industry closed down. For a time the *Telegraph*, the *Independent* and Mirror Group Newspapers were all in Canary Wharf at bargain-basement rates. What financial tenants there were negotiated startlingly attractive terms: their new landlords bought them out of existing leases in central London and offered them rent-free periods. To make matters worse for the brothers, the government went back on its promise to match the developers' investment in the new tube line and to relocate thousands of civil servants there.

Canary Wharf in the end turned out to have a catastrophic impact on the Reichmanns' business. They had assumed that there would never be simultaneous downturns in both of their main markets. By 1991, they were proved wrong. When the brothers were forced into receivership, the development ended up in the hands of the banks. The Reichmanns came back, however, with new financial partners; they went through a restructuring but they maintained their original conception for the nature of Canary Wharf, which in the end proved itself. It attracted the world headquarters of HSBC and the European base of Citibank. In 2005, when Barclays joined them, the development achieved a critical mass. Around it, the early industrial units were torn down, less than a decade after they were completed, to be replaced by larger office structures. More sites were acquired by Canary Wharf, and other developers began to build high-rise residential towers on either side of the office centre. At the beginning Canary Wharf was often seen as ersatz urbanism, a North American model transplanted to Europe, but it has become the pattern that others have followed.

London's boundary between affluent west and deprived east has been moving steadily eastward over the last 40 years. The financial district once stopped at Broad Street station. This Victorian obstacle was swept away when it was demolished in 1986, along with parts of the neighbouring Liverpool Street station, to make way for a complex of offices. Then the City leapt across Bishopsgate, which had acted as a development firebreak, into Spitalfields Market. 'Doomed and grimly magnificent,' was how the writer Iain Nairn described Spitalfields, with its Hawksmoor church and its streets of Georgian houses, in 1966. In fact, Hawksmoor's church and many of the Georgian houses are still there. Gentrification means that they are in much better physical shape than they once were. But the area has been overwhelmed by the city's financial industry moving east, and by the tourists who are attracted into the area by the energetic eruption of fashion-conscious art spaces, cafés and clothing stores. Truman's Brewery, one of the area's largest employers for two centuries, moved out 20 years ago. The site now has an owner who has understood that there is money to be made by doing as little as possible to the mix of industrial buildings the brewery left behind. Instead of redeveloping them, they rent the found space within them to café owners, galleries and a year-long round of pop-up market stalls and events.

The eastern edge of Spitalfields is Brick Lane, where what was built in the eighteenth century as a Huguenot chapel for French refugees from religious persecution, and which subsequently became a Methodist church and then a synagogue, is now a mosque.

Later, a 1960s office slab east of Brick Lane was transformed into the kind of workplace that is designed with a start-up economy in mind. The opening of Second Home, inspired by Rohan Silva, one time adviser to Downing Street on the digital world, was presided over by the Chancellor of the Exchequer, George Osborne. A few doors down, the pavements are still crowded with touts handing out flyers for curry houses, and shops selling saris. Inside Second Home, with its carefully selected collections of non-matching mid century modern furniture, and its curated evening events, is another world.

The Broadgate project, on top of Liverpool Street station, took an all-or-nothing approach like that of Canary Wharf, though without the need for high-rise markers. For Broadgate, the address was a particularly important issue. The contours of property values in the Square Mile are defined according to the precise boundaries of the city's four postal districts: EC1 to EC4. The London of E1, just a few feet away across an invisible line, was an entirely different world. This is one of the areas that the Victorian social reformer Charles Booth had mapped as the preserve of the 'vicious poor'. On one side were the solid masonry of the Edwardian banking palaces and the glass-curtain walls of more recent financial towers. On the other side were what the bankers still perceived as slums. There were offices to rent on both sides, but at prices that differed by a multiple of three.

Instead of using a high-rise to attract attention, the developer Stuart Lipton commissioned the American artist Richard Serra to make *Fulcrum*, a monumental steel installation, perhaps the single most powerful piece of monumental public art London has seen since the Charles Sargent Jagger war memorial in Hyde Park. And through some careful negotiation with local authorities, the whole development got an EC postcode when that section of the site, which had previously been part of the Borough of Hackney and in E1, was transferred to the postal jurisdiction of the City of London. Broadgate's 32 acres look like a city but, like Canary Wharf, are in fact private property.

There are pavement cafés and wine bars, offices and shops, a health club and plenty of public art. But never consider staging a political demonstration there, or even asking people crossing its granite plazas what they think about the quality of its architecture. Vox pop interviews are specifically prohibited in its guidelines for film-makers and photographers seeking permission to take pictures, consent for which, by the way, must be applied for at least two weeks in advance. Anybody ignoring this is liable to being stopped by the onsite security and handed over to the police.

The Broadgate Estate makes its strictly limited view of what constitutes a city abundantly clear:

> We cannot accept any filming/photography requests that fall into the following contexts: Religion, Racism, Sexual Nature, Political, Moralistic. Any competitor of our landlord and/or our occupiers. Disruption of the day to day business of the Estate. No filming/photography of any occupier's logos without the written permission of the relevant occupiers.

The combination of a City rattled by competition from the east, and an increasingly profitable Canary Wharf development, can be seen as the direct causes of the astonishing transformation of London's skyline in the last 15 years. It did not happen all at once. At first, Canary Wharf was a quarantined high-rise zone. The City of London had signalled that it was open to large-scale new projects. But it took time for it to deal with objectors to this idea of the future of the City. Several schemes were put forward, including a speculative proposal for an ultra-tall tower designed by Norman Foster that never materialized.

Then, at the end of 2001, after an extended public inquiry, came the decision of a planning inspector to reject English Heritage's bid to stop Gerald Ronson building the Heron Tower, a high-rise just east of Liverpool Street station. Opponents of the scheme argued that allowing it to go ahead would set an irresistible precedent and inflict serious violence on London's character and scale. And, as it turned out, they were right. It was an unequal battle. Neil Cossons, the chairman of English Heritage, had to fight the mayor, the developer Gerald Ronson, Peter Rees – a man who now lives in an apartment in a second tower nearby developed by Ronson – and the Commission for Architecture and the Built Environment, the government's watchdog on urbanism, chaired by Stuart Lipton, who had built Broadgate.

Shortly after the destruction of the two ancient Buddhas of Bamiyan in Afghanistan in 2001, Ken Livingstone was shameless enough to suggest that the Heron Tower's opponents were 'the Heritage Taliban' for trying to stop what he claimed was an investment in the future of London. Heron Tower turned out to be a 46-storey-high battering ram tipped by a decorative steel needle that tore its way through the fine print and the best intentions of London's planning system. The needle would have been even taller, but Ronson refused to pay for what he took to be the vanity of his architects. Consents for half a dozen other towers as tall or taller followed quickly.

Livingstone had been the leader of the GLC at the time of its abolition. He had taunted the Conservative government by posting a giant scoreboard on the front of County Hall in sight of Westminster, headlining rising unemployment figures. But even before he took office he had come to an accommodation with the City of London. With the City's advice, he adopted a strategy that was published as *The London Plan*. In essence it assumed that London was going to become the world's dominant financial centre, and the economic benefits from that role would include new jobs. The impact of half a century of population decline in London could be reversed and the City would be encouraged to grow eastward by investing in what was initially named Crossrail (before it become the Elizabeth line) and the post-Olympic development of Stratford. London's population, which reached a peak of 8.6 million in 1939, was down to 6.8 million in 1983. From this low base it had started to grow again, slowly at first, gathering speed in the years after 2001, putting on one million people in a decade, and regaining the pre-war level by 2014, well ahead of the plan's predictions.

This was a strategy that seemed in Livingstone's mind to depend as much on dramatic visual gestures as on scientific planning. If London was going to be an unchallenged global financial capital, it had to look the part. And in 2000, other international financial centres had skylines that looked like Shanghai or Beijing. London had set the pattern for Tokyo's nineteenth-century financial centre. Paris, as built by Napoleon III and Baron Haussmann, itself inspired by John Nash's work for the Prince Regent in London, was the template for Buenos Aires, Mexico City, Bucharest and a dozen other capital cities looking to import the latest incarnation of civic dignity. Now it is the cities of China that have become the models for ambitious cities trying to make a mark.

The global shift of economic and political power represented by the rise of Asia has a physical embodiment in the skylines of a dozen cities that have come from nowhere over the last 50 years. The warp-speed rise, first of Tokyo, then of Hong Kong, Kuala Lumpur, Taipei, Seoul and, above all, of Shanghai created a new urban model. In many cases these were symbolic representations. When much of the Western world had little idea of where to find these cities on a map, still less of what they looked like, conspicuous architectural landmarks were in many cases the first steps in a campaign to achieve brand recognition. These three-dimensional architectural advertisements were designed to attract attention and to provide a city with an instantly recognizable image, much as London has Tower Bridge and the Palace of Westminster and New York has the Chrysler and the Empire State. The twin towers built by the Petronas corporation do the job for Kuala Lumpur, and two ultra-tall towers facing each other across the harbour have come to symbolize Hong Kong. Shanghai has followed this strategy more than once in its history. The first version of the city is still visible in the stone façades of the Bund, Shanghai's colonial waterfront (fossilized through the Mao years), that looks like an uncanny transplant of a nineteenth-century European city to an Asian context. The second version was built at the end of the twentieth century when the city mutated from low-rise socialist squalor to brittle capitalist glitter in two decades. It was this Asian-accented version of a Western idea of urbanism that has now been re-exported back to London.

The transformation of the long-derelict acres of the Bishopsgate railway lands, the high-rises of Stratford, and the Greenwich Peninsula south of the Thames all demonstrate a scale and density that has its roots outside Europe. When the British took over the Chinese walled settlement of Shanghai and fought for their right to sell the opium that they cultivated in India to the citizens of the Chinese empire, there was nothing on what is now the Pudong side of the Huang Po River but a few shipyards and a seamen's hostel. Shanghai, behind the Bund, was never a conventional colony. The city was run by a series of different, but parallel, administrations with French, American and British concessions.

Skylines are the markers in a high-stakes competitive game in which Hong Kong (top), Dubai (above), Shanghai (opposite, top) and London (opposite) fight it out for global supremacy. There is always a new young gunslinger, ready to take on all comers to establish itself as more conspicuous, and more dynamic than the rest. It's a constant battle in which there is nothing more humiliating than being the city with a tower on its skyline that was formerly the world's tallest.

The British ran the police force, with European officers and Sikh constables. They shared control of the jail with the Americans. And along with the French all three issued driving licences.

It was an arrangement that allowed a hybrid culture to flourish in the cracks between regimes. In some parts of the city, it was never entirely clear exactly who was responsible for enforcing any kind of legal system. What is now the city's Zhonghua Road was once called the Boulevard de Deuxieme République and took you to Edward VII Avenue and Broadway. In those days you could have worshipped in your choice of onion-domed Russian Orthodox churches, the product of the army of White Russian refugees who sailed out of Vladivostok with the Bolsheviks at their heels. Shanghai in the 1930s was an island of floodlit art deco cinemas, neoclassical banks and electric trams, marooned in the midst of a China that had hardly changed in a thousand years. As the city petered out on the road to Nanjing, the neon signs and the street lights disappeared into the darkness of a medieval night.

The long freeze on Shanghai's development lifted only at the end of the 1980s, with the introduction of the market economy to China. With a population of around 20 million people, Shanghai is effectively a city state now, with the powers of the central government at its disposal to annex satellite towns and villages and to take open territory into its direct control. Those powers have been used to shape a vast new city. Shanghai created an elaborate idea of what it was going to be before it started on realizing its transformation. The first step in the process was the opening of the City Planning Museum. At its heart was a massive model of the colourful new Shanghai of the near future. The size of two tennis courts, it is ringed by multilevel walkways that allow visitors a view of the emerging new city from every angle. In the 1990s, it was the place that all new visitors to Shanghai came to see after the birthplace of the Chinese Communist Party not far away. At first the city it depicted seemed like the remotest of possibilities, a fantasy of steel-and-glass towers in the midst of a city in which open sewers still ran in the streets. In fact, the present-day skyline is even more frenzied in its wild architectural imaginings than the model in the museum promised.

The Oriental Pearl Tower, a cluster of spheres impaled on a concrete tube, like some fantastically naive idea of an interstellar spaceship standing upright, ready for blast-off, has been overwhelmed by a ring of ever taller high-rises. The first of them to take shape was the Jin Mao Tower, with allegedly oriental geometries, topped by a hotel, with a vertiginous atrium at its core, as portrayed in a famous photograph taken by Andreas Gursky. Next door is the Japanese developer Minoru Mori's tower, which took longer to complete than planned after the perceived symbolism of the original design ran into political trouble. It had a tapering, squared-off top, pierced by a void in the form of a perfect circle. For the Chinese this seemed to suggest that the Japanese sun was rising over their city once again as it had during the Second World War. Mori initially responded by proposing to fill the void with a Ferris wheel. At 101 floors above ground, it would not have been an experience for the faint-hearted. Eventually, the tower known as the Shanghai World Financial Centre was realized in somewhat tamer form as a giant knitting needle with an open slot at the top. The Shanghai Tower at 632 metres high, with 128 floors, is even taller. Its twisting form demonstrates a challengingly convincing impression of instability.

Shanghai has the most assertive of skylines, which must be understood as an attempt to bulldoze itself into the list of essential world cities. At night it ripples with neon and light-emitting diodes like *Blade Runner* brought to life. Smog permitting, during the day it presents a distinctive silhouette of towers that is instantly recognizable as the symbolic incarnation of the new Shanghai. Towers are symbols but they are also a vital step in achieving substance. 'Pay attention' is the message of all those towers. Build them and the bankers will come.

Before the wave of new building really took hold, Shanghai staged an architectural competition to find a development strategy that would turn the whole Pudong area into the city's new business district. The process, and the result, showed both the strengths and weaknesses of Shanghai's position. Many of the world's leading architects – Toyo Ito from Tokyo, Massimiliano Fuksas from Rome and Richard Rogers from London among them – were invited to take part. They all put forward more or less radical attempts at master-planning, all of them mutually exclusive in their approach to land-use and form, that all turned out to be more or less irrelevant. Richard Rogers produced an ecologically inspired diagram for a city based on mass transit and bicycles that had a curious echo of Ebenezer Howard, the nineteenth-century British originator of the garden city concept. Ito and Fuksas were more formal. The city claimed to have adopted the best features of all the competitors, and the development of the new business district in Pudong proceeded at breakneck speed, although along lines that bear little resemblance to anything that emerged in the competition.

Shanghai was determined that every visitor knew the scale of what was going on, and harangued them in language that recalled the days of the Red Guards. Carved in both Chinese and English into a low granite wall were the words: 'Persist in the development of Pudong without wavering until it is done.' But in the Bund, the most recent architectural signifier of luxury and status is now the insertion of minimalism behind the carefully conserved façades of the imperialists. Shanghai is beginning to adopt a more nuanced attitude to its own past, or, as a former mayor urged his citizens, 'Rejoice in the present, while recalling the past.' At the regional level, Shanghai is developing a policy for its position at the centre of the Yangtze delta. It has embarked on the construction of a ring of satellite towns – designed in German, Italian, Scandinavian and Chinese urban styles. On an international level, it is competing with Singapore and Tokyo. It is moving beyond manufacturing to advanced service industries, such as software design, finance and fashion, as much a part of the rhetorical agenda for every ambitious city as culture-led renewal. Shanghai now has its own Disneyland and a neighbouring retail theme park.

Shanghai is a city that has been through a spasm of change so violent that it tests the limits of human resilience. In the 20 years after 1990, living space per person in Shanghai doubled to reach 15 square metres per resident. In the same period, the city built 40 per cent more roads. In 2004, there were nearly two million cars. Six years later, there were 3.5 million, and the city started to try to curb further increases by issuing quotas for the sale of new cars. The first section of the underground metro system opened in 1993. It reached a daily capacity of more than 10 million at the end of 2014. Shanghai is still working to reduce population densities in the inner city, where there are particularly crowded areas such as the Old West Gate, with people living at 1,800 to the acre – much like Mumbai's Dharavi – by moving them to far-off suburbs.

Development in Beijing followed the pattern set by Shanghai. It built its own museum of city planning, a suave six-storey structure faced in black glass close to the southern end of Tiananmen Square. One wall of the entrance is dominated by a vast bronze relief map of Beijing as it was in 1949 when the People's Liberation Army made its triumphal entry. You can still see the Forbidden City where Mao spent his first night in a pleasure palace, in a style that his Imperial predecessors would have recognized, surrounded by Confucian texts. The Gate of Heavenly Peace, from which Mao declared the foundation of the People's Republic with the ringing cry that 'the Chinese People have stood up', also survives. But there is not much else left of the city lovingly depicted in miniature in the vast model that forms the museum's main attraction. Mao mutilated the ancient fabric of the city to carve out the megalomaniac scale of Tiananmen Square. He had mile after mile of the city's ancient walls, and the gates punctuating them, demolished. The destruction took a decade of laborious and futile handwork. Mao built the Great Hall of the People and the Museum of the Revolution, two huge hulks, on either side of Tiananmen, which are little compensation for what was lost. They were carefully aligned on the axis of the Forbidden City that still defines Beijing, to claim the legitimacy of China's Imperial past for the People's Republic. But Mao's buildings were also big enough to eclipse the palaces to demonstrate the superiority of his own regime.

The main draw in the planning museum is on the top floor: a vast model of the new Beijing. You approach by walking over a series of photographs taken from surveillance satellites that show you the city fringes. Lit from beneath, and protected by thick sheets of glass, it gives you the sensation of flying over Beijing's suburbs. It's a disorientating prelude to the city centre that is modelled in detail. China was once a command-and-control economy. And the new Beijing, which has come into being in the past three decades, shows that in its fabric. Immediately west of Tiananmen Square, hundreds of courtyard houses were flattened to build the national opera house, an inscrutable glass-and-titanium egg designed by Paul Andreu, a French architect specializing in airports. It has five different auditoriums and seats 6,500 people. Almost by accident the area to the east of the city centre became the focus of a seemingly random sprouting of high-rise towers. They are here because this is where the embassies were built when the Communists moved the diplomatic district away from the city centre into what were fields in the 1950s. It was the obvious place to build the first international hotels and the commercial towers.

The first time I went to Beijing was in 1992. There were no direct flights from London then, and the airport felt like a cold, unheated provincial bus station, with hard wooden benches. Its Sino-Stalinist architecture suggested the intimate connection between air travel in China and Party privilege. Flickering black-and-white television screens signalled departures with erratic imprecision, and a kiosk selling Napoleon Brandy in bottles shaped like vintage cars, costing a worker three months' pay, stood in lieu of a duty-free shop. The two-lane road into town was clogged with carts bringing in mountains of winter green vegetables to feed the city. And Beijing, once you finally got there, went dark after 9 pm. Change, when it came, was stunningly swift. It took just four years to build the brand-new airport that Beijing opened in time for the Olympics of 2008. It is larger than all the terminals at London's Heathrow put together, but it was designed, built and opened in rather less time than the lawyers spent arguing about Heathrow's Terminal 5. (It is not surprising that the experience of building it left its architect, Norman Foster, frustrated at Britain's inability to make up its mind what to do about its lack of airport capacity in London. It also got him the attention of Boris Johnson when he proposed the construction of an entirely new airport for London in the Thames estuary to replace Heathrow altogether.)

Beijing was conceived of as the most modern and best-equipped airport in the world. But building it was an operation on a scale that came close to the massive nineteenth-century urban projects that saw the rise of the first industrial cities. It looked like a medieval battlefield, conceived on the scale of a Japanese epic film. Swarming warrior armies clustered around giant cranes, more than 100 of them, at one point, ranged like ancient siege engines across a front line almost two miles long. The dust swirling across the landscape made it impossible to count more than a few of them before they disappeared into the acrid haze. The banners flying from makeshift flagpoles sunk into the mud everywhere carried the names of individual work gangs, each with their own territory. The gangs moved like disciplined cohorts of soldier ants, identifiable by the colour of their helmets, navigating blindly but effectively around the obstacles that littered the site. Some were handling new deliveries. Others were preparing them for use. Yet others shifted barrowloads of nuts and bolts or carried steel bars by hand to where they were needed. In the foreground, groups of men in crumpled suits stacked heaps of reinforcing steel, ready to be bent into the hooks that kept them securely in place when they were finally buried in concrete. There were dumps of steel everywhere. So much steel, in fact, that it was only too clear how the Chinese hunger for the metal pushed up world prices to the point that British constructors rediscovered the art of building in concrete. There was enough steel there to explain why Australia reopened abandoned iron-ore mines, and why shipbrokers took bulk carriers out of mothballs from their anchorages in the Fal estuary. (Equally it explains why, with the pace of Chinese development tailing off in 2015, commodity-based economies are all in trouble now.)

The significance of Beijing's airport is not simply the role that it plays in shifting large numbers of people in and out of the city. Just as important is its part in the conspicuous assertion of a new kind of China and its modernity. But at the precise moment I was there, however, the project seemed to belong more to the past. To the recent past of Mao, and his control-and-command economy, as well as the more distant past of the Industrial Revolution and the Europe of the nineteenth century, with its own frantic construction boom. Or, despite the steady stream of China Eastern Airbuses rising in quick succession from the active runways serving the existing terminal, the even more distant past of the ancient Chinese dynasties.

The site worked in three shifts, seven days a week. Nothing

stopped the cranes, the concrete mixers, the welders and the scaffolders. Not even the discovery of fossilized dinosaur bones that turned up in the mud ahead of the bulldozers one day, or a beautifully carved ancient stone, saved from the mechanical diggers and re-erected next to a cluster of huts. The workers here stopped only for the Chinese New Year, when it got too cold for concrete to set properly, and the site came to a standstill as the armies returned to their villages until the thaw came. During the day they braved the dust storms and the summer heat. At night they worked under arc lights. They slept in ramshackle clusters of huts and green army tents, in a series of shanty towns scattered around the runway. The huts varied in size and shape. Some were made from plywood, with corrugated clear plastic sheets to form the roofs. They were held down by bricks to stop them from blowing away. There was no glass in the windows, and nothing more elaborate than roofless huts of latrine blocks for sanitation.

These men were the twenty-first century's version of the navvies who built Britain's railways and its canals. They were the legal, the semi-legal and the illegal migrant workers, drawn from China's desperately poor hinterland in their millions by the prospect of jobs in construction and in the factories that the booming cities of China had to offer. At a certain point it was estimated that one in every five of Shanghai's population of 20 million was an illegal migrant. Beijing was not far behind. These migrants were Chinese citizens with fewer rights in their nation's capital than Colombians living illegally in California. Everywhere you went in Beijing in the run-up to the Olympics, there were clusters of spray-painted numbers scrawled over walls, on trees and gateposts, under flyovers and on lamp posts. In Compton or Harlesden they would be gang tags. But there was no graffiti in China then. They were the mobile phone numbers of people looking for work. On the way out to the airport, you could start to spot them long before the site gates. Just a few numbers and a single Chinese character were enough to describe their owner's individual skills and how to reach them. Or, in some cases, nothing more than blank strings of numbers.

When he became London's mayor, Ken Livingstone went to see China for himself. He saw what he took to be the future of the modern world and went home with such an enthusiasm for skyscrapers that he made the construction of the Shard – yet another attempt at Europe's tallest tower – possible by directing his employees at Transport for London to rent 10 floors of office space inside it, transforming the up-to-then fragile finances for the project. In the event, office values rose fast enough for TfL to make a profit when they were bought out of their lease before the project was completed. Their signature on the lease had done its job. It made the development look credible enough to the banks to finance the project. Despite his incendiary past, Livingstone appears to have modelled himself on a combination of big-city American mayors of the stamp of La Guardia, with a touch of the imperial style of François Mitterrand thrown in, rather than the more restrained British tradition of municipal public service. It is inconceivable that a Labour traditionalist local council leader would do what Livingstone did and earmark £100,000 from the Greater London Authority's budget to defend in court his personal choice of sculptor for a singularly lifeless tribute to Nelson Mandela. Nor would such a figure ever have claimed that it was his duty as mayor to lead rather than to listen; a destiny manifest in his decisions on everything from questions of aesthetics to the extension of the congestion-charging zone westward.

When Michael von Clemm made his first visit to Canary Wharf all those years ago, there was a national consensus in Britain that, after the disastrous bulldozer-rampant years of the 1960s, you did not build tall buildings in historic city centres, you did not demolish working-class communities based in old but serviceable Victorian terraces, and you did not sacrifice individual historic buildings to make way even for work by fashionable contemporary architects. Almost without noticing, the status quo has been reversed, not because of a single compelling vision, or an idea of what a city should be, but from the messy reality that is the context in which cities are built. For a city, practice can be more significant than theory.

Despite the apparent solidity of London's masonry, concrete and brick crust, a congealed surface on a molten core in transition, London is as fluid now as it has ever been. In 1984, it took nothing more challenging than an insignificant extension to the National Gallery, less than 100 feet tall, to goad the Prince of Wales and his supporters to such a fever pitch of fury that, 30 years later, the architectural profession has barely recovered. Thanks to the Prince, London lost the chance of a Mies van der Rohe tower a year later. It was planned to have just 18 storeys, at which height it would have been dwarfed by the skyscrapers that have sprouted in the City since then. The Prince went on to try to stop the project that replaced Mies's design, James Stirling's Number One Poultry, which is itself now a candidate for listed-building status. Today, most of London, from Stratford in the east to Wandsworth 15 miles west, is caught in the path of an unstoppable juggernaut of redevelopment fuelled by cheap money and the profits to be made in London's property bubble that can be derailed only by Britain's self-inflicted departure from the European Union. There are plans for at least three towers that will be over 1,000 feet high, which have sparked little mainstream political debate despite the re-emergence of radical activists such as Occupy and Class War.

Undaunted by periodic downturns, each new project looks bigger and more wilful than the last. Construction on one high-rise tower got no further than the first few floors of the lift core before the credit crunch of 2008 stopped work. Five years later a new owner decided to demolish it and start again on an even bigger tower on the same site. New projects arrive in a rush of computer-generated renderings and are immediately pushed off the news agenda by the next huge project. Far from trying to cool things down, the government's advisers charged with safeguarding architectural quality, the Commission for Architecture and the Built Environment, stood by and applauded. As the boom gathered speed, CABE concentrated on ensuring that architects it approved of got to build them. Richard Rogers and Norman Foster, Jean Nouvel, Rem Koolhaas and other architectural celebrities benefitted from this policy. 'The City certainly won't draw a line that says people can go this high, and no higher,' CABE's deputy chairman at the time, Paul Finch, said. 'Developers believed that they stand a better chance of getting planning permission if they use a good architect, and that is leading to the kind of architecture we are seeing now.' He did not reflect on the fact that CABE's first chairman was Stuart Lipton, himself a developer, whose forced resignation in the wake of complaints of conflict of interest revealed the essential contradictions of his position.

When CABE was set up by the Blair government, London was recognizably the same city that Canaletto had painted. It had the dome of St Paul's at its centre. The tallest new structure, now called Tower 42, known as the NatWest Tower when it was completed, was an isolated one-off. But now London has sprouted Europe's most conspicuous high-rise downtown, or, perhaps more accurately, two or even three of them: one at Canary Wharf; another around Bishopsgate in the City; and a third concentration of residential towers around Vauxhall. Not even the unsentimental planners of Moscow have allowed high-rises into their city centre, let alone those of Paris.

Large parts of London have turned into a free fire zone for developers. Sometimes it seems as if they couldn't quite believe what was happening, and they were daring a reaction, playing a game of grandmother's footsteps to see just how much they could get away with. 'They can't possibly roll over and take this one seriously,' you can almost hear them thinking, 'but we do.' The tallest building in Europe? Yes, please, said both Ken Livingstone and Boris Johnson. An even taller tower? Why not? say the city planners. Can we build the Vauxhall Tower, tallest block of flats in Europe, the block that the planning inspector wanted to turn down because it wrecks the view of the Palace of Westminster? Yes, said the government minister who overruled him.

The argument for high-rise offices in London is made on the basis of a perhaps mistaken, but at least plausible, policy. The case was never argued for the private residential towers that are now lining the river from Putney to Greenwich and, on an even greater scale, are threatening to spill into the west, as Renzo Piano's proposal to reprise the Shard with an equally tall residential skyscraper on top of Paddington station suggested. It is these projects that reflect the way in which London's very success is threatening to undermine it; they are a visible reflection of the emergence of London property as an asset class rather than as a means to provide affordable homes for its people. In the context of interest rates at their lowest in a century, and quantitative easing, property has become a place to launder money, to look for windfall gains from price inflation, rather than a place to live.

The blowback from the property explosion has made most London property unaffordable for all but the wealthiest of its residents; threatening to choke off the city's ability to attract the young and gifted who have been responsible for so much of its recent success. The edges of Canary Wharf are now defined by a thicket of high-rise residential towers, with more coming in Stratford, on the Greenwich Peninsula, and a particularly egregious single file of towers lining the route from Old Street roundabout to the Angel. They provide a skyline in constant transition, characterized sometimes by forests of tower cranes, marked at night by red aircraft-warning lights. At other moments in the construction cycle, the extraordinary sight of a cluster of slender 50-floor-high toothpick-thin concrete lift shafts, before they have disappeared to form the cores of undistinguished residential towers, is a moment of short-lived visual excitement.

It is in the east, and also south of the river, that investment-led housing in London has experienced its most luxuriant growth. Who knows what would have happened to the stretch of the Thames between Vauxhall Bridge and Chelsea Bridge if, shortly before it stopped generating electricity, Battersea Power Station hadn't become famous for the starring role that it played on the cover of Pink Floyd's album *Animals*? In the days before digitally manipulated artwork, creating the image involved actually making a giant inflatable pig and cautiously floating it between Battersea's four giant chimneys. The album turned a piece of industrial archaeology – with a spectacular art deco interior – into a popular landmark.

It was designed in the early 1930s by Sir Giles Gilbert Scott. He belonged to an architectural dynasty that made an indelible mark on London. His grandfather Sir George Gilbert Scott was responsible for the flamboyant Gothic St Pancras station. The younger Scott designed Britain's cast-iron red telephone boxes, Waterloo Bridge and, most conspicuously, two power stations on the Thames. The one at Bankside, with just a single chimney, is now Tate Modern. Battersea, a huge brick cliff, was by far the most imposing landmark on the south side of the Thames west of the old County Hall, and would very likely have been demolished after 40 years of working life, a relic of London's vanishing industrial past.

For 30 years, Battersea was the Bermuda Triangle of London's property market. A succession of developers would sweep in, famous architects in tow, sink fortunes into what they assumed would be a prime riverside site, and then, one after another, disappear without trace. First up was John Broome, who managed to persuade Mrs Thatcher to unveil his plan to make it into a theme park: 'a little bit Disneyland, in a far more English way', he suggested and produced plans that showed Charles Dickens Street, the Battersea

Tavern and an incongruous collection of high-tech white-knuckle rides. Broome got not much further than taking the roof off and dismantling the turbines before running out of cash. Battersea was left to rot. With no protection from the rain, it turned into a ruin.

Part of the problem was image. Battersea and Vauxhall, for those who did not know it, seemed impossible to get to, and marooned in a tangle of railways and dereliction. Worse, it was the wrong side of the Thames. For centuries Londoners went south of the river either to behave badly (the pleasure gardens of Vauxhall were notorious), to dump rubbish or to pursue the kind of trades that were considered too much for the more refined north.

What really turned the tide for this stretch of the river was the decision of the US to move its embassy from Grosvenor Square to a more security-conscious new building midway between the power station and Vauxhall Bridge. Even when it is fortified against truck bombs, an American embassy is a more upmarket neighbour than the homeless shelters, gay nightspots and parcel depots that characterized the livelier parts of the area in the 1990s.

Battersea finally took off when a wider plan was drawn up that tried to coordinate all the vacant sites between Vauxhall and Battersea known collectively by the planners, but not by anybody who actually lives there, as VNEB (Vauxhall, Nine Elms and Battersea). It is a vast area comprising 195 hectares, in the hands of 13 different owners. A new pedestrian bridge across the Thames is planned to make it more accessible and an extension to the Northern Line tube system is underway. There are now 16,000 homes and enough work space for 25,000 jobs in the pipeline. They are being built in three clumps.

To the east, Vauxhall has already sprouted one residential tower 600 feet high and which is the first of four more residential towers that will be almost as tall. One is luridly Versace-branded and the sales pitch concentrated on suggestions of an instant profit when the building is complete in 2017, sure-fire signs of a crash in the making. All it takes is a deposit of just 5 per cent now and you can expect a capital increase of £230,000 on a £1 million apartment before it is even completed.

The second clump is more modest in size, and takes in the zone around the American embassy. This section on the river is designed by Richard Rogers's firm, Rogers Stirk Harbour + Partners, and takes the form of a series of parallel glass-and-steel slabs, angled to give Thames views to as many flats as possible. The power station itself is now owned by a Malaysian consortium, which has bet Malaysia's pension fund on the third zone, and packs in 3,100 apartments, 1.5 million square feet of offices, and a retail centre. More than 800 flats were sold off-plan in a feeding frenzy of buyers from all over the world attracted by blistering house-price increases in London before Brexit brought sales to a standstill. London's new neighbourhood – if that is what VNEB will be, and its apartments bought as investments don't sit half empty – is like nothing the city has ever seen before. The ranks of skyscraper apartments are exactly what Londoners told themselves they did not want to allow in their city.

Could it have been done any differently? Was there another way that London could have secured its place as the financial capital of the world without making itself look like Shanghai? La Défense in Paris is the French attempt at building a financial centre. It is the product of a very different process since it remains a state-controlled project: the product of an imperial presidency. The result is a cluster of towers, built above a shopping mall, that are apparently not so different from Canary Wharf. Rather than adopting London's expediency, it is an attempt at making a grand statement through the continuation of the axis that starts with the former royal palace of the Louvre and continues along the Champs-Élysée, through the Arc de Triomphe and then a further four miles on out to La Défense, an area that was a bedraggled suburban edge to the city, of scattered development, makeshift houses and even a few fields right up until the 1950s. De Gaulle set up a state organization, known by its acronym EPAD, to develop the area as a business district, an approach that continued when the Mitterrand administration held an architectural competition to crown the axis with a new, inhabited monument, known as the Grande Arche. Mitterrand, as heir to the Sun King, was prepared to have the whole neighbourhood shut down one weekend for the largest crane in Europe to be manoeuvred into position to hoist a beam to the height of the Grande Arche so he could see for himself how it would look from the garden of the Élysée Palace.

The Grande Arche duly got built, even though its purpose was sketchy, other than for some windy rhetoric from Mitterrand about it becoming a place for dialogue between outer and inner Paris. It was filled with civil servants, despatched by government fiat, public access to the viewing gallery is no longer permitted for safety reasons, and the skin itself has shown an alarming tendency to shed tiles. On the other hand, the government did put the RER mass transit system linking Paris's historic centre with its suburbs in place at La Défense before the main offices were built rather than afterwards, as has happened with London's Crossrail. And Paris had no alternative power base to sabotage the project in the way that the City of London did with Canary Wharf. With so many of the commanding heights of French industry and commerce at least partly state-controlled, the president was in a position to insist that they move to La Défense. It is inconceivable that France would allow ownership of the development to pass into foreign hands in the way that Canary Wharf did. Continuing in the imperial way of French planning, Nicolas Sarkozy's son was appointed to run the EPAD, though he stepped down after questions about what other credentials he had to do the job apart from being his father's son. La Défense had housing as part of the plan from the beginning and 20,000 people lived there early on, but it was generally seen as a bleak environment with no real connection to the offices and the commercial centre.

London has tended to shrug off attempts to tame and direct its growth ever since its citizens ignored the efforts of Tudor monarchs to prevent the spread of suburbs outside its city walls, and its refusal to accept Christopher Wren's master plan for its reconstruction after the Great Fire. Its rush westward was given a massive, and entirely unintended, boost by the random creation of a heavy bomber aerodrome at Heathrow that later became Europe's largest airport. And the Great Lurch East of the 1990s, represented by the eruption of the Canary Wharf, was an equally pragmatic development. Certainly London has had large-scale urban visions in the past. Nash built the Mall, Haymarket, Piccadilly Circus and Regent Street on a scale heroic enough to inspire Napoleon III to remodel Paris, just as it was the London Underground that used to set the pace for the Paris metro. The Barbican, London Wall and Paternoster Square were the products of carefully considered planning strategies, not all of which proved successful in the long term. But in most of its history London has changed and grown through pragmatism more than by design. Through a mixture of ruthless opportunism, unintended consequences and political turmoil, London has developed as fast as any Asian city in the past decade.

Cities feed off each other for ideas. Once Asia's cities started to grow, it was inevitable that an ambitious European city should seek to match them. What could not have been predicted is that the conjunction of a left-wing Labour mayor with the financial markets and property developers would come together to outwit Paris and Frankfurt to establish London as a global financial capital. In retrospect, the Livingstone and Johnson mayoral terms managed an impressive job on transport: Peter Hendy will go down as a leader at Transport for London who equalled if not bettered the pre-war achievements of Frank Pick. But the utter failure to build adequate affordable housing has threatened the whole nature of what has made London attract the ambitious, the gifted and the young from around the world. London has done badly at building housing other than as speculative products for investors looking for a new asset class. It has demonstrated that it is incapable of taking some key transport decisions, such as how to expand its airport capacity, but it has done a remarkable job of upgrading its Victorian train lines, to create the Overground network. How much longer this imbalance can be left unaddressed is open to doubt.

If office rents are a measure of the attractiveness of a district, La Défense and Canary Wharf are equally unappealing for the business elites of their own cities, with 2015 rents a third of more well-favoured areas. But Canary Wharf is still as expensive as the costliest offices in Paris, suggesting that it has more international appeal. From the point of view of France's national ambitions to create Europe's leading financial centre, La Défense cannot be said to have succeeded as well as Canary Wharf, which began with much more modest objections. As a piece of urbanism, La Défense has greater pretensions to civic qualities, and yet it is just as much a reflection of the confrontation of a bubble of affluence within a deprived suburb. In understanding the nature of the mechanisms of urban change, the comparison between the effectiveness of pragmatism set against a more formal approach to planning is as much a reflection of national identity as it is of the philosophy of development.

With Britain's vote to turn its back on Europe in the referendum of 2016, the relative effectiveness of these contrasting approaches will be put to the test. The vote to leave was forgotten Britain's retribution on a capital city so pampered that Boris Johnson and George Osborne were prepared to squander £160 million on a garden bridge while local authorities in the north could not afford to keep their museums open. And the exclusion of the City of London from the Euro Bond market that may follow will be Paris and Frankfurt's chance to take its own revenge.

Chapter Four

The Government of Cities

Walt Disney was a man who was fascinated by cities. He put a lot of thought and energy into the possibility of creating something that would amount to more than the 5/8th-scale facsimile of Main Street USA that he built in California in 1955. He wanted something that didn't close every night after Disneyland's visitors had been escorted off the premises when the firework display had finished. He wanted something real.

Disney is the man who could be said to have infantilized the world through the perspective of a mouse. But there were aspects of his personality that suggested a more worldly version of Buckminster Fuller, the guru of the geodesic dome, dymaxion engineering, and who coined the term 'Spaceship Earth'. Disney also had the focus and the resources to turn his own speculations about the future into physical form in a way that Fuller found to be harder going.

Both Disney and Fuller believed that it was possible to treat a city as if it were an elaborate machine and to design it around the complex systems – energy, water, movement – that would sustain it. Fuller was fascinated by the idea of putting a protective bubble over Manhattan. After Disney's death, his successors at the corporation made a geodesic dome the centrepiece of a future-based theme park in Florida.

Before he turned his attention to urbanism, Walt Disney had already worked with Robert Moses, the ruthless civil servant who was New York's planning overlord for four decades. Almost the last act of Moses's time in New York was the staging of the 1964 World's Fair. Disney designed the General Electrics display and inspired the General Motors Pavilion. It was an unabashed hymn to the car and the freeway, a celebration of the power of robotic machines to cut through forests and hillsides, spitting out fragments of timber and rock to leave behind smooth black tarmac roads. The collaboration between Disney and Moses was one of the more unlikely relationships of the twentieth century. Disney, who had no schooling after the age of 15, changed the nature

Buckminster Fuller wanted to save the city by destroying it – by building a bubble over Manhattan (top). Walt Disney's Main Street (bottom) is another kind of retreat from the world, a nature reserve for the city where lost fragments of urbanity have been stitched together like Frankenstein's monster, and are protected from reality by a fence and a ticket office.

of popular culture. Moses, a graduate of Yale and Oxford, was to New York what Haussmann had been to Paris.

Haussmann was the civil servant that Napoleon III imported from the French provinces. His primary task for almost 20 years was to build the new boulevards that would give Paris the imperial splendour his patron craved, and, in the process, to destroy most of the remains of medieval Paris. Haussmann set about it as if he were conducting a military campaign. He commissioned an immense 1:5,000-scale map of Paris, almost 15 feet long and 9 feet high, which he distributed throughout his staff. He kept his own engraved copy constantly on hand in his office, mounted on a specially made rolling stand, like a general on the eve of battle.

Haussmann was the Prefect of the Seine. Moses was also a public servant, with a collection of much more obscure job titles, of which the Chairmanship of the Triborough Bridge and Tunnel Authority was the most influential. Moses never held an elected office, but nevertheless he built New York's bridges and parkways, its housing projects, municipal parks and public beaches. It was Moses who cleared the way for the United Nations to come to New York, and who made the Lincoln Center possible. His influence spread far beyond the city into New York State through his control of the state park system and its hydroelectric dams.

Unlike Haussmann, he never depended on the patronage of a single powerful political champion. Moses accumulated power through a ruthless understanding of how every level of New York government worked, and a careful cultivation of the press, which for years presented him as a champion of progress and lauded his ability to secure Federal funds for the city. Moses was the kind of public servant who ended up holding the public, and the representatives that they elected, in contempt. 'There is nobody against this – nobody, nobody, nobody but a bunch of mothers,' Moses protested when Jane Jacobs began her campaign to stop him driving a highway through Washington Square Park and through

Chapter Four

Robert Moses's last act in four decades of driving roads through New York and building massive housing and cultural complexes was the 1964 World's Fair. It was a bombastic vision of urbanism that united Walt Disney, Henry Ford and Moses in a single photo opportunity (above), as they prepared for their nine-minute tour of Moses's vast model of New York City in their moulded-plastic tracked-car.

The vast panorama of the City of New York, commissioned by Robert Moses for the World's Fair, is now on show at the Queens Museum. It was advertised as an indoor helicopter tour, and documented the city that Moses had actually built. Progressland (overleaf) was the Disney version.

VISIT...
PROGRESSLAND
a WALT DISNEY presentation
at the 1964-65 N.Y. World's Fair
Great in '64, GREATER in '65

Jane Jacobs, the journalist turned activist, stopped Moses's bulldozers in their tracks. Even more significant was the manifesto that she wrote, advocating a more sensitive version of urbanism than big-picture planning.

Greenwich Village, which he attempted to have designated as a slum, and building a ten-lane expressway through Lower Manhattan. He believed he knew best about the kind of city that was needed. Mayors and governors came and went. Moses went on year after year, fuelled by the tolls that his officials collected from the bridges and tunnels that he controlled, and the patronage that went with the contracts to build them that were in his gift.

Haussmann was also able to offer his allies the chance to make fortunes. While not personally corrupt, his enemies claimed that details of which properties were to be compulsorily purchased, and generously compensated, to make way for his schemes were made available before they became public. He demolished large areas of Paris, but he left behind a city the rest of the world took as a model of urbanism. Moses's legacy was more conflicted. For Jane Jacobs, who wrote *The Death and Life of Great American Cities* as an outraged response to what Moses was doing to New York, and in particular his plans to drive a highway through Greenwich Village, he was the Great Satan. She looked at the results of what Moses called 'urban renewal', his 'slum' clearances in the Bronx and the West Side, and found that whatever his claims to the contrary, its real effect was to undermine poor but stable neighbourhoods.

Moses had clashed with New York's cultural elite even before he encountered Jacobs. In the run-up to the 1964 World's Fair, he had insisted that *13 Most Wanted Men*, the mural commissioned from Andy Warhol by the architect and former Museum of Modern Art curator Philip Johnson, be painted out because he objected to its content depicting criminals on the run from the FBI. Johnson rejected Warhol's offer to replace the portraits with 13 new ones of Moses. But the Fair did offer such attractions as the installation of Michelangelo's *Pietà* in the Vatican Pavilion, where it could be viewed from a moving travellator.

Walt Disney was impressed enough by the Fair to hire Moses's engineer, William Potter, to work on EPCOT, the Experimental Prototype Community of Tomorrow that he planned to build in Florida. General Motors was brought in to create a car attraction that would help to pay for the project. Disney had wanted to build what he claimed would be a model city for 20,000 people, equipped with schools and businesses as well as homes. Monorails would provide public transport, cars would be relegated below ground, leaving the surface for pedestrians, a standard element of 'radical' thinking about cities that was still visible 50 years later when Abu Dhabi set about building Masdar, its experimental green city, which initially banned cars and provided an underground world of robot-driven taxi pods.

To judge by Disney's rhetoric he wanted EPCOT to offer an answer to Jane Jacobs's anxieties about the future of cities. For all the new affluence and the superficial confidence of the 1960s, there was a profound unease in America and Britain that the physical fabric of the city, apparently so reassuringly solid, seemed to be permanently on the edge of putrefaction. Apparently healthy urban tissue could be destroyed by even the most trivial infection that would turn once-healthy streets into slums. Disney was determined to do it differently. 'There will be no slum areas because we won't let them develop. There will be no landowners and therefore no voting control. People will rent houses instead of buying them, and at modest rentals. There will be no retirees; everyone must be employed.' What Disney did not see was that creating a city was more complicated than building a university campus, a hospital or a business park. While a holiday resort might have some of the ingredients – places to work, eat, sleep, shop and learn – in the end, it is not a city. None of them, Haussmann, Moses or Disney, ever understood or believed in the essential role of democratic government in the making of a city and in its day-to-day functioning. Without democratic accountability, there is no scrutiny of objectives, or their achievement.

There is no chance to reflect on the aspirations of the poor or the marginalized, or to ensure that public money is spent honestly.

Walt Disney never got to build his city, but the Disney Corporation that he founded has been involved with planning and building real streets in real towns – if the word 'real' has a meaning in this context – since the first Disneyland opened. Shopping malls in Los Angeles, the revitalization of Boston's Quincy Market, and Silicon Valley office complexes all have a debt to Disney's expertise and his ideas about the street and the pedestrian, in one way or another.

The Disney Corporation of the Michael Eisner years appeared determined to breach the gap between mainstream taste and high culture. It had Robert Stern, one time Dean of the Architecture Faculty at Yale, as a board member. Michael Eisner took Robert Venturi and Denise Scott Brown, authors of *Learning from Las Vegas*, and a troupe of other high-powered architects on a weekend retreat to talk about strategy for the new theme park that he planned to build outside Paris. Eisner eventually ended up looking at architectural portfolios from practically every important contemporary architect. Rem Koolhaas, Jean Nouvel, Michael Graves, Aldo Rossi, Frank Gehry and a dozen others were all asked to make detailed proposals – a sign of the increasing sophistication of Disney's audience.

Of all these names, perhaps the most exquisite of ironies is the inclusion of Aldo Rossi on the list. Rossi would have driven Senator McCarthy to apoplexy. McCarthy would undoubtedly have suggested that Disney was promoting un-American activities. Rossi was a Marxist, and a long-term member of the Italian Communist Party, who tried to bring poetry to urbanism with his reflections on the place of memory in cities. Despite Rossi's politics, Michael Eisner was determined to persuade him to work for Disney. Rossi in the end accepted a number of commissions. They did not go well. A timeshare holiday resort in Newport in the form of a Mediterranean village with a ruined Roman aqueduct running through it came to nothing. Rossi resigned from another project at Euro Disney in frustration at his client's interference. 'I am not personally offended and can ignore all the negative points that have been made about our project at the last meeting in Paris,' Rossi wrote. 'The Cavalier Bernini, invited to Paris for the Louvre project, was tormented by a multitude of functionaries who continued to demand that changes be made to the project to make it more functional. It is clear that I am not the Cavalier Bernini, but it is also clear that you are not the King of France.'

The only project that Rossi designed for Disney that was actually built was in Celebration. It is hard to be sure exactly what to call Celebration, the 7,500-resident community that the Disney Corporation created after the death of its founder. The word 'village' is used about it a lot. But perhaps the most pitiless description of a development with architecture by America's leading postmodernists Michael Graves, Robert Stern and Charles Moore among them, but with no public transport, is that it is 'Designated as a place for the purposes of the US Census.' Rossi designed a complex of three distinct office buildings for Disney's imagineers. Based on the form of the Campo Santo in Pisa, they are grouped around a lawn with an obelisk at its centre, and are embellished with fragments of classical architecture. In the context of Florida, it is a space that has the surrealistic dreamlike quality of a de Chirico painting.

Rossi was fascinated by the way that the monuments built by ancient cities survive and mutate over time to shape contemporary life. In the backstreets of the Tuscan city of Lucca, for example, you come across an oval open space, ringed by tenements that are built into the Roman walls of what you gradually realize was once an amphitheatre. In the Croatian city of Split, Diocletian's palace survives, trapped like a fossil within the modern city, with buildings from every succeeding epoch grafted to the walls of ancient Rome.

Rossi tried to find ways in which such layers and resonances could be replicated in new developments and cities that have no such backstories. He found clues in the unlikely setting of East Berlin in the simplified classical forms of Karl-Marx-Allee that seemed to Rossi to maintain the essential sobriety of a dignified monumental city put to work, as he noted, for the proletariat rather than the bourgeoisie.

In his book *The Architecture of the City*, Rossi suggested a new way of understanding the city, which he described as the 'collective memory of its people'. According to Rossi,

> One can say that the city itself is the collective memory of its people, and like memory it is associated with objects and places. The city is the *locus* of the collective memory. This relationship between the *locus* and the citizenry then becomes the city's predominant image, both of architecture and of landscape, and as certain artifacts become part of its memory, new ones emerge. In this entirely positive sense great ideas flow through the history of the city and give shape to it.

Earlier in his book, Rossi defines the *locus* as 'a relationship between a certain specific location and the buildings that are in it. It is at once singular and universal.'

Despite its roots in Marxist analysis and structuralist philosophy, Rossi's ideas about the city as the collective memory of its people have much in common with Disney's fascination for America's Main Street USA as a reminder of a shared past. And so might have had an appeal for Disney.

In their different ways, Rossi and Disney were both skilled at using design to trigger memories, associations and emotions. By reflecting the forms of a traditional European city in the midst of the Florida landscape in his offices for Disney, Rossi was hoping to give them a certain dignity and urbanity. But while the work of both the imagineers and Rossi is pictorially convincing, it lacks substance. Just as a theme park can have the appearance of a city, with none of its essential layers of meaning, so Disney was trying to make something that is as complex as a city simple enough for him to be able to keep control of it with some of the same techniques that he used on Main Street: choreographed pedestrians, dress codes for the help. But oversimplifying a city means that you strip it of everything that makes it function as one. A place that deals with the issue of poverty by evicting people who lose their jobs – as Disney suggested he would do – is no city. That is something the British Conservative politicians who deny housing benefit to those families living in areas deemed too expensive for the public to support them in would do well to think about.

You can see the same process of oversimplification at work in the privatization of parts of the city. There are urban developments in which the pavements, apparently public spaces, are not in fact public at all. They are spaces that are not maintained or policed by the city around them; they remain in private hands that discourage skateboarders and picnickers, and politics. And yet, in the midst of clumps of skyscrapers, and alongside major pieces of public infrastructure, these spaces have every appearance of forming part of the public realm.

Cities are the urban equivalent of artificial intelligence. You start with the most basic circuits that simply distinguish between on and off, or between building and absence of building. As you add more and more components, you can eventually build something that comes to a semblance of life: a digital chess player that will beat a grand master; a car that can drive itself. So the accretion of urban ingredients – the house, the factory, the warehouse, the airport, the bus station, the hotel, the bookshop, the ice rink, the shop, the theatre – eventually creates something that transcends the ingredients. Building/non-building may yet become a square, piazza, forum. Complex cities have the diversity that gives them their extraordinary ability to renew and reinvent themselves. Simplified cities have a coarser grain, and they lose that agility and energy. When streets are overwhelmed by out-of-town shopping malls; when affordable social housing is out of balance with homes built for sale to overseas investors; when workshops migrate to remote business parks, the city is being simplified. Oversimplifying a city means that you don't fix an ailing shopping centre, you simply abandon it and build a newer, bigger mall elsewhere.

The ways in which capital is used to finance urban development militates against the build-up of the complex urban fabric on which resilient cities depend. Developers work with simplified chunks of building: simple enough so that they can pitch the same package to bankers in London and New York and Tokyo. To raise finance from around the globe for a city project, the elements of an investment need to be understood by people who have never been there. Those elements need to be in a part of town that the prospective investors can understand from their own experience; they need to have the kind of tenants that can be understood, with the buildings and the mix of uses that can be understood. A Hyatt hotel or a shopping street running all the way from a Burberry store to a Louis Vuitton conveys the same message anywhere in the world. The ambition involved in staging the Football World Cup or building a Guggenheim museum is understood in every context. Canary Wharf in London and the World Financial Center in New York are examples of such simplified slices of city. They can look urbane enough, with solid granite façades, public fountains and a convincing mix of shops and apartments and offices, but they bear the same relationship to an authentic slice of city (which is necessarily complex, not simple) that a Starbucks does to a family-owned Italian café.

Starbucks is designed to process something efficiently – reasonably palatable coffee – and deliver it in what is essentially a simple way anywhere in the world. The Starbucks system is good design in the sense that a Kalashnikov rifle is a piece of good design. It is cheap, reliable and idiot-proof. In terms of investment in the city, it works – initially at least. When the funding is in place, the returns are there in capital appreciation as well as rental for the funder. But money applied in this way makes cities work that little bit less well. They lose some of their diversity, they lose authenticity and a bit more of their extraordinary ability to renew and reinvent and regenerate themselves, like dying coral atolls in the Indian Ocean. And in the long run, it leaves the capital that has been invested in them at risk too.

Like Stanley Kubrick's astronaut forcing open the pod door, pulling the plug on HAL and turning the sentient, self-aware computer back into a frightened pocket calculator as more and more circuits shut down, so a city turns back into a feudal village, or Disney's Celebration or even Silicon Valley. A city needs a form of organization that allows its citizens the maximum freedom to do whatever they want, without negatively impacting on others. These are freedoms that require institutions strong enough to be able to protect them. To ensure the individual feels safe, a police force that can be held to account is needed. To allow a city to flourish, to attract talented newcomers and to make the most of the talents of its existing people, a city needs a successful education system that is open to all. A city needs to find ways of housing its people, ensuring their health and giving them the means to move easily around the city. It needs some sort of planning system that will prevent the creation of toxic waste dumps next to residential streets.

Exercising such powers has often been the starting point for larger political ambition. Juscelino Kubitschek was the Mayor of Belo Horizonte before he was the President of Brazil. Turkey's President Recep Tayyip Erdoğan built his political reputation as Mayor of Istanbul.

Strong central governments often find power in the hands of cities troubling. France, for example, has abolished the post of

Mayor of Paris twice for lengthy periods: once for over 50 years from 1794 to 1848; and again for more than a century from 1871 to 1977. At Celebration, the Disney Corporation took care to ensure that the residential part of the development was separated administratively from the rest of its land holdings to safeguard Disney's powers – to do as it liked inside the Magic Kingdom – and ensure they were not diluted by neighbouring homeowners.

Forms of government have a direct impact on how cities work, and even how they look. This is the subject of Siena's most famous mural, *The Allegory of Good and Bad Government*. It took the fourteenth-century Italian artist Ambrogio Lorenzetti most of 1338, and some of the following year, to complete. It fills three walls of the handsome room in Siena's Palazzo Pubblico, the town hall, in which the Council of Nine, the oligarchs who governed the Sienese republic for most of the fourteenth century, met to deliberate on policy. This was the room in which they oversaw the construction of a series of aqueducts to bring water into the city, planned Siena's prison policy, regulated its bankers and created an education system.

The city that Lorenzetti painted might seem impossibly far removed from the present-day concerns of, say, Beijing's residents, fearful for the health of their children in a city in which the pollution is so thick on many days that it makes it impossible to see from one side of a street to the other. But his work covered the walls of the room in which, week after week, the city had to consider how to deal with the outbreak of plague that killed one in every two of its citizens, very likely including Lorenzetti himself.

The twenty-first-century version of the council still meets in a room in the same building, when its members can fight their way through the line of tourists waiting to climb the 400 steps of the Torre del Mangia that rises above it. The mural is art of the highest quality, but it was also conceived as an instruction manual, an inspiration and as a piece of civic propaganda.

Good government gets pride of place, and Lorenzetti made the city that was created by such a system look wonderful. The Council of Nine would have faced it from their seats every time they met. They were shown what they could achieve – a beautiful city, full of life – and offered the tools that they needed to do the job – a commitment to justice and public service. Bad government is represented as an awful warning, crowded into a single wall, the one which has been most damaged over the centuries by flaking plaster. It shows the city empty of life and partly in ruins. The fields outside the walls have been abandoned. It is a terrible prefiguration of the plague that swept through Siena 10 years after Lorenzetti finished his work. Though much of the allegory is complex, full of occult meanings and allusions to the Renaissance's rediscovery of Aristotle's ideas on ethics and politics, it is also a startlingly modern reflection of the most fundamental fears and hopes that every contemporary city still faces. The painting expresses the issues in terms as clear and powerful as a political speech made by one of the generation of reforming Latin American mayors such as Enrique Peñalosa in Bogotá, who cleared the city centre of cars and invested in public services in deprived suburbs, and Jaime Lerner, who brought cheap and efficient dedicated bus lanes to Curitiba in Brazil. It is an implicit criticism of those who see the city as nothing more than a place to enrich themselves, for private profit. This was as much a feature of fourteenth-century Siena as of twenty-first-century Los Angeles, Moscow or London.

It is a reproach to a Republican America that concluded there were no votes to be had in the cities and turned its back on them. And it is a message for those affluent suburbanites reluctant to pay the property taxes that will support the downtowns that they fear and despise, and who agitate to have themselves unincorporated.

The messages of the mural are still startlingly relevant even if Siena itself seems to have forgotten them. Corruption in the twenty-first century at the Banca Monte dei Paschi di Siena, the oldest bank in the world, set up by the city in 1420 and now its

Ambrogio Lorenzetti's paintings challenged Siena's fourteenth-century political class to maintain the rule of law against the tyranny of corruption. Virtuous government (above) brought prosperity and civic values. Without it came disorder and decay (opposite).

biggest employer, has undermined the institution whose vanished profits were used to sustain the city's cultural and social programmes – even the annual Palio horse race in the central square – and a variety of philanthropic activities.

The allegory may not seem immediately relevant in the *favelas* of São Paulo, where adolescents join street gangs for protection from police death squads. But the question that the painting asks – how a city can guarantee the security of all its citizens to ensure their prosperity rather than act only in the interests of a few – is relevant everywhere. The answer is a civic society based on a self-governing community rather than a self-defeating focus on individual gain. Siena had a well-organized police force and penal system in the fourteenth century. It understood that the safety of its citizens, and the security of their property, could be guaranteed only by the rule of equitable laws, administered without self-interest. Enforceable laws depend on a perceived sense of justice. When justice ruled with equity, reason and moderation, the city flourished. Lorenzetti's scenes celebrate such a city. There is dancing and music in the streets, cobblers are making shoes in their workshops, masons are busy putting up new buildings, and the shops are full. Citizens who seem to be students sit quietly listening to a lecture – there had been a university in Siena for at least 100 years before Lorenzetti started work on the mural. The countryside beyond the city gates is rendered with all the artist's skill to suggest a lush landscape, where the groves are full of fruit, corn is ripening and the flocks flourish.

Bad government, represented by a tyrant with the features of the devil, displays nothing but contempt for Justice and the law and shows the evils of violent lawlessness. The tyrant is motivated only by selfishness and greed, which in turn brings with it a breakdown in civic order. The houses are turning into decayed slums. There is arbitrary arrest without due process; there are brigands and muggers in the countryside, burning crops and looted houses. These are startlingly modern lessons that the scandal-hit cities of today's more corrupt regimes could learn from. It is a rebuke to the bribery that robs cities of their infrastructure to the benefit of private pockets. It is an argument for the obligations of the individual to the community, but also for the legal protection of the individual and his property.

The chaotic recent history of Mexico City stands as eloquent witness to the havoc that a corrupt system causes. It has endured a sequence of self-inflicted civic disasters that is the product of a system in which corruption and self-interest have eaten away at the foundations of government and the law. Violence is used as a tool to protect the interests of the powerful. Corruption in pursuit of short-term gain has cost many lives. Those who stand in the way, judges and lawyers as well journalists and politicians, have been bribed, intimidated and murdered.

A fire in the 1980s at the vast mountain of rubbish at Iztapalapa burned for days and engulfed the entire city in a toxic milky-white cloud that made the streets unendurable for more than a week. The fog that settled on every part of Mexico City forcibly brought home both to the wealthy and the marginalized the terrible cost of a failure to put in place a functioning refuse-disposal system as well as the corruption that had allowed the Iztapalapa catastrophe to happen. The smoke cloud was followed, a couple of years later, by an explosion at a state-owned liquid gas plant on the northern edge of the city. Illegal squatter settlements had grown up dangerously close to the gas tanks. When they blew up, flames and shrapnel ripped into the nearby shacks, taking 500 lives. After these two catastrophes came an even worse tragedy for Mexico City: the 1985 earthquake that killed at least 5,000 people, victims as much of inadequately enforced building codes as the tremors themselves. Mexican politics finally emerged from seven decades of monopoly power in the hands of the Institutional Revolutionary Party in the late 1990s. Mexico City gained a directly elected mayor, greatly strengthening the role of civic society in the government of the city.

Corruption has damaged Moscow in a different way. It has made it a dangerous place in which to do business, and it has littered the city with sites that mark deals that have soured. Yuri Luzhkov, a former mayor, became notorious for the way that he ran the city. In 2010, he was removed by the Russian Prime Minister, Dmitri Medvedev, after Muscovites spent the summer choking on smog caused by peat fires and stuck in unprecedented traffic jams. In one of the many scandals that have changed the face of Moscow, Luzhkov had presided over a tender that gave Shalva Chigirinsky, a flamboyant developer, the right to take on the sprawling site of the monstrous Brezhnev-era 3,200 room Hotel Rossiya ahead of two other bidders. It stood on the remains of medieval Moscow, immediately next to the Kremlin, wiped out in Stalin's time to make way for what was meant to be the last of the city's crop of wedding-cake skyscrapers. Instead it was used to build Europe's largest hotel.

Chigirinsky, originally from Georgia, trained as a doctor but by the end of the Soviet era had moved into property speculation. His principal asset was a substantial stake in Sibir Energy, a highly profitable London-based Russian oil company. At one point *Forbes* magazine put his personal fortune at $2.3 billion. In 2008, Chigirinsky had three massive projects underway. He wanted to make the site of the hotel into a kind of Covent Garden for Moscow. He had plans for building the Rossiya Tower, which would have been the tallest skyscraper in Russia. And he was also working on a vast entertainment complex on the edge of the city. All three schemes depended on his connections to succeed. The key relationship was with Luzhkov's wife, Yelena Baturina, who is still the richest woman in Russia.

According to *Forbes*, Baturina and Chigirinsky both had offices in the same Moscow building that was also occupied by the city's department of development and architecture, the authority that had granted planning consent for the Rossiya Tower. However, the projects were hit not only by the worldwide credit crunch, but also by the souring of Chigirinsky's relationship with Baturina, and with her husband, the mayor. By the end of 2008, Chigirinsky was on the verge of leaving Russia. One of the unsuccessful bidders for the Hotel Rossiya site had gone to court to contest the tender process, claiming that Chigirinsky, who had bid only $830 million compared with his own offer of $1.4 billion, had insider knowledge of the transaction. The project ground to a halt. Putin eventually approved a plan to turn it into a park. Work also stopped on the 600-metre-high Rossiya Tower project. 'Say thanks to Alan Greenspan and George Bush,' Chigirinsky suggested sarcastically. Chigirinsky had become overextended financially. He had borrowed $325 million from Sibir Energy, a loan that had not been disclosed to the other shareholders and which caused a scandal when it was revealed, leading to a £350,000 fine for the UK-based company chairman, Henry Cameron, who resigned. Chigirinsky's attempt to sell his property assets, including the Kremlin site, the high-rise and a St Petersburg project, in 2009 to Sibir for $433 million (far more than they were worth) was blocked. Moscow City Council, which had a stake in Sibir Energy, successfully fought the attempt to dilute its value that the purchase of Chigirinsky's property assets would have represented.

When intimate connections between government and the oligarchs are added to a lack of an impartial legal system, a city's future is compromised. For a time, Russia encouraged the development of a civic society. Environmental activists and advocates of open government have played a part in ensuring that Moscow has started to address some of the issues that face it. Public spaces have been upgraded, but the traffic jams are still severe. Its remarkable architectural heritage is still under threat.

These shortcomings are not limited to cities that share Moscow's authoritarian political structure. Dealing with them effectively is more likely in those cities which attempt to follow the traditions of civic government established in Siena. Manchester town hall, built almost 700 years later, is a recognizable descendant of Siena's Palazzo Pubblico. It was built to accommodate an emerging form of democratic local government. It has a swaggering clock tower and a picturesque skyline of serrated gables to demonstrate civic ambition. The explosive growth that turned Manchester from a small town into the birthplace of the Industrial Revolution began in the second half of the eighteenth century. The town became a corporation in 1833, and a city, in the official sense, only in 1853. The building of the town hall began 15 years after that, and was only completed in 1877 in a struggle to catch up with a city that had already exploded. Manchester was a city before it had a government. We cannot know how differently it would have grown if the government had come first.

Ford Maddox Brown's sequence of huge murals inside the great hall is a blithe celebration of Manchester's triumphant progress – from its origins as a Roman fort to the building of the Bridgewater Canal, by way of Danish invasions and the arrival of Flemish weavers – rather than an argument for good government. But just as the Sienese republic self-aggrandizingly traced its roots to ancient Rome, so Manchester, and the other industrial cities of northern England, identified with the prosperous city states of Italy.

This is where the young Norman Foster began work as a trainee in the Treasurer's Department in 1951, long before he decided to become an architect. Manchester town hall was designed by Alfred Waterhouse, who was perhaps the most prolific architect that Britain had produced (until Foster eclipsed him). Waterhouse pierced the endless corridors with complex staircases that provide glimpses across multiple levels, a riot of polished granite and chiselled representations of thirteenth-century Gothic. The decorative detail had a story to tell: there are bees – the symbol of the city – represented in the tiled ceilings, and stone ridges are cut to look like ropes of woven cotton, reminding Mancunians what it was their city had been built on. In the entrance vestibule, you find the incongruous spectacle of Early English-style vaulted ceilings, lit by polished brass electric chandeliers.

Manchester's town hall represents a form of municipal government that is no longer fashionable in Britain. It was built for a very particular kind of administration: a city corporation that was ready to take on every aspect of the well-being of its citizens; transport as well as water, power and sewers, housing as well as schools; services that were delivered by paid officials, answerable to a council of elected politicians. They carried out their duties without payment, and so needed to have private means. The mayor was a ceremonial figure elected by the councillors, and political direction came from the leader of the council, a figure subject to party discipline. The leader's authority came not from a personal mandate, but from the votes gained by their party. It was a paraphrase of Westminster government, with a ceremonial head of state, a prime minister and a civil service. There was no upper chamber, but the division of power with other tiers of government had a restraining effect. The city's employees included architects to design the homes that it rented to those of its citizens that needed them, engineers who built its roads, administrators who planned the curriculum in its schools and who decided which university courses would attract grants for its young students, and street cleaners and teachers.

It is a model of civic government that has lost its appeal since the assault on centralization by the Conservatives that began with Margaret Thatcher's administration. Local authorities no longer have the funding powers to build homes on their own account, and their tenants were given the right to buy their homes. Under both Tony Blair and David Cameron, local authority involvement with education has also been minimized. Street cleaning, refuse collection, parking controls and transport have been largely subcontracted to private companies. Shorn of these responsibilities, local authorities have cut back on their employees. Just as both Conservative and

Labour Westminster administrations restricted the ability of local authorities to deliver services, both parties have become interested in the idea of directly elected mayors to revitalize cities. London was the first, and was judged to be a successful experiment. During the term in office of both Livingstone and Johnson, London grew at what seemed like the expense of the English provincial cities. In David Cameron's second term, the Conservative strategy was to devolve power to the northern cities. In 2015, a briefly ascendant Conservative chancellor spoke of creating a northern supercity for England, based knowingly or unknowingly on some of the thinking of the maverick architect Cedric Price in the 1960s with his idea of a Potteries Thinkbelt, a university distributed throughout the industrial north. The Conservatives are pushing for city government of the kind embodied by London's first two elected mayors, Ken Livingstone and Boris Johnson. Sadiq Khan, elected as third mayor in 2016, suggested London's commitment to cosmopolitan tolerance.

In exchange for adapting government systems to directly elected mayors, Manchester, Leeds and Sheffield would get more control of local government spending. The rhetoric amounted to a recreation of what the Northern Powerhouse cities had been in their great days, when Waterhouse built his town hall. But while London's mayoral system has certainly built an impressive transport system, it is no better at offering Londoners affordable housing than any other English city. The balance of powers between these layers of government varies from country to country. India ensures that its cities never become dominant by keeping them subordinated to state governments and to New Delhi. In America, and much of Europe, mayors have substantial power.

In Britain, a central government concerned about spreading the capital's wealth more evenly around the country is reluctant to allow London too much financial autonomy. The city has to counter the arguments of those outside London that see the capital sucking in more than its fair share of investment in infrastructure of all kinds. Investment in transport infrastructure is heavily weighted towards London, The first Crossrail line connecting Heathrow in the west with Stratford in the east will be followed by a north–south line. The High Speed 2 (HS2) rail line will connect London with Birmingham and Manchester, mainly to the benefit of London. London's airports are privileged ahead of those in the rest of the country. The Arts Council and the Department for Culture, Media and Sport spend more per head on opera houses, museums and theatres in London than in the rest of England. This investment has contributed to the overheating of London's economy, but given the way in which power and influence on a global scale are concentrated in fewer, larger cities, it has also played an important part in maintaining Britain as a whole in the international picture. London generates the wealth that subsidises the rest of Britain. If London is eclipsed by Berlin as a centre for digital innovation, Frankfurt supplants it as a banking capital and Paris acquires a better-connected airport, it won't be to the benefit of Birmingham or Edinburgh.

Norman Foster had the chance to design London's new City Hall. It symbolizes this new approach to government as much as the Manchester building in which he once worked does the old. Tellingly, London's City Hall belongs not to Londoners, but to the property company that built it, the product of the early twenty-first-century mania for private finance for public work that initially looked thrifty but proved enormously expensive in the long run. The London Assembly's 25 elected members could have been accommodated in an anonymous office building with no recognizable public face. It would have been presented as the financially responsible option, but it would have left London's government invisible and lacking any sense of the kind of presence on which authority is based. With its eccentric form – Ken Livingstone called it a 'glass testicle' before he became London's mayor – the new City Hall gave British municipal government a makeover. It was like cricket being given the baseball treatment. No more English whites; the old game is played out now under floodlights and the players wear lime-green pyjamas. In the case of City Hall, democracy has been given a background of purple carpet and yellow walls that looks good on television, and a celebrity mayor debating under TV lights with little chance to be called to account by the assembly between elections.

The London that is now emerging was shaped in the interregnum between the old Greater London Council, as it was propelled to the scrapheap when there was no strategic planning authority, and the Labour administration that, when elected in 1997, established the Greater London Authority. London today is the product of any number of conflicting forces. Without a coherent government for more than a decade, a period in which there was little public faith in the positive impact of planning, London has emerged as the product of financial calculation and the consequences of technological change. It has been a test bed for the stream of fashionable planning prescriptions that have spread around the world with the speed of avian flu. It has become the city that nobody expected it to be, and which nobody willed it to be. It is the outcome of countless individual wills, of political expectations and of economic shifts of capital from Asia, the Arabian Gulf and Russia to London. It has a democratic government, but one that essentially does not give its citizens more than the power to turn out an administration every five years. It is not a Swiss city that can choose to ballot its citizens on anything from a veto on the building of minarets, or the design of an art gallery, to the ownership of second homes.

Few people in London knew that in electing Livingstone and Johnson they had voted for a skyscraper city. Nobody voted to have a housing stock that was priced grotesquely beyond the means of the majority of its citizens, although it is clear that most of its homeowners would not have been happy about any politician trying to do anything that, as they would see it, might cause the value of their properties to fall.

The choices that a city can make are not generally susceptible to a 'Yes'/'No' alternative on a ballot paper. Instead, city politicians choose their ground carefully. The price of a ride on public transport is crucial to their electoral prospects. When education is under the control of a local authority, it shapes the political debate. In theory, communities like to see controls placed on what can be developed next door to their homes, but individuals do not care to have such restrictions placed on themselves. Many of the questions that have the biggest impact on a city – the location of an airport, the route of a railway, mortgage rates – are made elsewhere. Ever since Jane Jacobs started her successful campaign to stop Robert Moses, it has been through activism and campaigning on individual issues, from cycle lanes to conservation, that citizens have their most immediate part in shaping their cities. Jacobs ignited a wave of popular protest against planning and planners in the 1960s and 1970s that was not confined to New York. Paris fought, albeit unsuccessfully, to stop the destruction of the old markets of Les Halles, and London did save the fabric of the old Covent Garden from destruction to make way for new roads, even if the vegetable market itself was relocated to Nine Elms. Jacobs's view of the city shaped the thinking of activists and city planners almost until the turn of the twenty-first century. She believed in the pedestrian scale and what she called the 'ballet' of the street, of mixed communities in which there was a balance between the long-established and the incomers attracted by the qualities of a dense city centre. She characterized the results of Moses-style planning as the antithesis of all the things that she and so many people love about city life.

But in the face of the massive expansion of Asia's cities, Jacobs's approach seemed inadequate to the challenge of formulating a response in the West. She was unclear on how to protect a city from its own success, from the market forces that drive up retail rents in once-attractive but run-down areas. She had little to say on how to avoid the worst effects of the process of gentrification. She did not talk about what could be done to break the cycle that saw artists moving into gritty but potentially attractive streets inevitably being followed by art galleries, then by restaurants and bars, which in turn inevitably seem to attract the fashionable and the affluent so that the artists have to move out.

It is not just road-building plans by car-obsessed politicians that make it impossible to buy a pint of milk or a spanner or a bag of nails in Belgravia, London, or in Chelsea, New York. It is property taxes and rent premiums. It is distribution systems and the lack of affordable city-centre housing to accommodate the people who drive the trucks that deliver the stock, and the buses that get the people who sell the stock to work. When a frivolous mayor of London (Boris Johnson), backed by an equally frivolous Chancellor of the Exchequer (George Osborne), agree to spend £60 million on a garden bridge in London, its not surprising that some people outside the city vote to leave the European Union to poke that metropolitan elite in the eye.

Using planning restrictions and inducements to achieve even the most worthwhile objectives – whether it is to protect pubs and corner shops from being displaced by new tenants able to afford the higher rents that follow gentrification, or discouraging the use of cars – backfires. Very often, it has produced the unintended consequences that are the exact opposite of the outcome that was hoped for. Rent-controlled apartments in New York have turned into subsidies for the already relatively privileged rather than a way to keep nurses and bus drivers close to their jobs. Mexico City's efforts to restrict car use by introducing odd- and even-number-plate-only days predictably led the wealthy to buy a second car. In the 1960s, a Labour government in Britain had tried to cool London's office-building boom by rationing the approval of more office space. The expectation of scarcity pushed up the value of office space, and had the result of creating more offices than would otherwise have been built.

The enlightened management of privately owned urban estates

It takes trauma to make a complacent city invest in its future. The cholera epidemics of the nineteenth century forced London and Paris to build sewers. For Beijing (above) toxic air quality has forced an autocratic regime to respond to the fears of its people. In Moscow the smoke cloud of 2014 got the city mayor the sack.

that are nevertheless built around public spaces has done a better job of keeping city centres alive. When a private landlord sees a slice of city more like a farmer viewing his fields rather than as a conventional property developer appraising a site for a quick return, they see the long-term benefits of a mixed community in terms of its attractiveness and sustainability. London's family estates have maintained control of large areas of the city for centuries. The most successful of them have worked to attract the variety of users that supports the vitality of an area.

Gentrification so far has almost always been a one-way process that has had the effect of sterilizing an area. Once a multi-occupied house has been turned back into a single home, further shifts in ownership are rare. The exception is in retail property. When tourism overwhelms an area, retail patterns are inverted. Instead of offering the luxuries that characterize city-centre shopping, souvenir stalls, selling in enormous volumes, drive out everything else. However, Covent Garden, like Les Halles in Paris, went from adventurous to tawdry; and then the enlightened self-interest of its owners saw a renewed attempt to create a better balance of tenants.

Like everybody else, planners tend to use the tactics of the last war to fight the battles of the next one. Southwark today is presented as a model of urban good practice, studied by envious planners the world over looking to emulate its strategy of culture-led urban renewal, based on the success of Tate Modern in transforming perceptions of the area. Two decades ago, and with equal commitment, Southwark believed that it had a duty to protect the way of life of its threatened communities. And to create, or defend, what it saw as the kind of employment that would bring 'real' jobs to the community. It wanted to stop warehouses being transformed for cultural use.

The lessons of Siena's allegory can be used to guide an approach to urbanism that has more to offer than the hermetic bubble of Walt Disney's sterile plan for EPCOT. A city is too complex a system for the market to function on its own to deliver desirable results. The market cannot deliver adequate quantities of affordable housing unaided, as London's current crisis, not much different from New York or San Francisco's or a dozen other affluent cities, demonstrates. Cities are shaped by the sometimes random interactions of individual ambition, of the checks and balances of politics, and of legislation. A city is shaped by managing water resources, economic policy, transport planning and law enforcement, as well as issues that are usually presented as being at the softer end of the scale, such as making public spaces that people want to spend time in. Making a city work is about encouraging racial tolerance through education and the fairness of policing. It's about creating a civilized public transport system.

Politicians love cranes; they need solutions within the time frames of elections, and cranes deliver them. But there is only a limited number of problems that are susceptible to this kind of time scale. The result is a constant cycle of demolition and reconstruction that is seen as the substitute for thinking about how to address the deeper issues of the city. Visions for cities tend to be the creation of the boosters rather than the theorists or the policy-makers. City builders have always had to be pathological optimists, if not out-and-out fantasists. Cities are made by an extraordinary mixture of do-gooders, bloody-minded obsessives and cynical political operators and speculators. They are shaped by the greedy and the self-interested, the dedicated and the occasional visionary. Those cities that are stuck, overwhelmed by too much rigid, state-owned social housing, or by economic systems that offer the poor no way out of the slums, are in trouble. A successful city is one that makes room for surprises. A city that has been frozen by too much gentrification, or too many shopping malls, will have trouble generating the spark that is essential to making a city that works. The cities that work best are those that keep their options open, that allow the possibility of change. They depend on the kind of democracy that involves more than voting.

Chapter Five

The Idea of a City

Friedrich Engels is not the only writer to have looked over the edge of the abyss in fascinated horror at a city in the midst of what seemed like a shocking mutation, and grip an audience with his account of what he saw. Charles Dickens explored a London lost in the fog, smoke and mud of its struggle to become a modern capital, with its broken legal system, debtors' prisons and child criminals. Dickens famously opens *Bleak House* with his startling invocation of 'a Megalosaurus, forty feet long or so, waddling like an elephantine lizard up Holborn Hill', with which he so powerfully captures the sheer sense of strangeness of a vast city in the midst of violent transition and the idea of a modern city sinking in mud that seemed to be dragging it back to a primordial swamp.

In *Dombey and Son* (1846–8) written just after Engels's *The Condition of the Working Class in England*, Dickens described the coming of the railways slicing through the streets north of King's Cross, leaving whole houses dangling in mid-air.

> The first shock of a great earthquake had, just at that period, rent the whole neighbourhood to its centre. Traces of its course were visible on every side. Houses were knocked down; streets broken through and stopped; deep pits and trenches dug in the ground; enormous heaps of earth and clay thrown up; buildings that were undermined and shaking, propped by great beams of wood. Here, a chaos of carts, overthrown and jumbled together, lay topsy-turvy at the bottom of a steep unnatural hill; there, confused treasures of iron soaked and rusted in something that had accidentally become a pond. Everywhere were bridges that led nowhere; thoroughfares that were wholly impassable; Babel towers of chimneys, wanting half their height; temporary wooden houses and enclosures, in the most unlikely situations; carcases of ragged tenements, and fragments of

> unfinished walls and arches, and piles of scaffolding, and wildernesses of bricks, and giant forms of cranes, and tripods straddling above nothing.

Forty years later, Émile Zola portrayed life in nineteenth-century Paris and the impact of Napoleon III's extraordinary, if flawed transformation of the city. *Au Bonheur des Dames* is set in a department store in the 1860s, one of a fast-modernizing Paris's more recent urban innovations that would be imitated around the world. The department store was a place in which the newly affluent acquired the tastes of the aspirational classes. They learned what to wear, which fork to use and how to furnish their homes. Zola introduced his readers to an institution modelled on Aristide Boucicaut's Le Bon Marché store, which still occupies much of the Rue de Sèvres. It used innovative architecture to create a wildly popular indoor space for the public that summed up modern Paris.

> But opposite, the gas-lamps were being lighted all along the frontage of Au Bonheur des Dames [. . .] The machine was still roaring, active as ever, hissing forth its last clouds of steam; whilst the salesmen were folding up the stuffs, and the cashiers counting up the receipts. It was, as seen through the hazy windows, a vague swarming of lights, a confused factory-like interior. Behind the curtain of falling rain, this apparition, distant and confused, assumed the appearance of a giant furnace-house, where the black shadows of the firemen could be seen passing by the red glare of the furnaces. The displays in the windows became indistinct also; one could only distinguish the snowy lace, heightened in its whiteness by the ground glass globes of a row of gas jets, and against this chapel-like background the ready-made goods stood out vigorously, the velvet mantle trimmed with silver fox threw into relief the curved profile of a headless

woman running through the rain to some entertainment in the unknown of the shades of the Paris night.

Later, the store induces a Haussmann-like official to give it a grand frontage on one of Paris's new boulevards.

Even if Engels could not match Dickens or Zola for literary quality, the robust directness with which he wrote *The Condition of the Working Class in England* invented a new way of looking at cities; one that has continued to resonate. His book is an impassioned assault on the class system. It is also a close reading of Manchester, an extraordinary city – though still not yet officially designated as one – in the midst of a traumatic birth. New wealth was being created by a range of new technologies, while the poor, who provided the labour that made them possible, lived in squalor. The impact of the new industries could not be confined to what happened inside the factories. They needed new people, who needed places to live, and a new city grew up around the mills. Some areas of Manchester were little more than barracks. But many of the mill owners were keen to celebrate their wealth and to assert the prestige of their city with a civic building programme. There were new churches, libraries and schools. The railways and the tram networks took shape.

While Engels's main objective was to expose the malign effects of capitalism, he was a sharp enough observer to see more than exploitation. He noticed that Manchester's centre emptied at night quite unlike any other city he had known. There was little sign of life after dark but for the lights of the watchmen guarding their employers' property. Manchester was an early version of the doughnut city, a type that became common in the 1960s. When a city centre turns into an office ghetto, it becomes depopulated and, as a result, rich and poor live increasingly segregated lives. The very poor stayed close to the old city centre, while the affluent moved further out when suburban railways made it possible.

A century later, in a process described by the American writer Alan Ehrenhalt as the 'Great Inversion', the doughnut effect went into reverse. In a gentrified city, the poor are still segregated, but they have been pushed out of the areas in which they once lived into deprived suburbs, while the affluent have returned to colonize the centre. Life in a distant suburb where transport depends on a private car can be even more difficult for those on a minimum income.

Engels looked at the physical form of the city, at buildings and streets and landscapes. But, like Dickens and Zola, he was also fascinated with the people in those streets. He noticed what they wore: broadcloth for the wealthy, fustian for the rest; what they ate and drank and smoked. The poor had to put up with adulterated food, often it was all that they could afford.

Above all, Engels wanted to see how the working class lived. He took his readers on an indignant journey through the lower depths of degradation that was kept out of sight of polite society as much as possible. He provided a vivid report from the front line of an urban explosion.

> First of all, there is the Old Town of Manchester, which lies between the northern boundary of the commercial district and the Irk. Here the streets, even the better ones, are narrow and winding [. . .] the houses dirty, old, and tumble-down, and the construction of the side streets utterly horrible. Going from the Old Church to Long Millgate, the stroller has at once a row of old-fashioned houses at the right, of which not one has kept its original level; these are remnants of the old pre-manufacturing Manchester, whose former inhabitants have removed with their descendants into better-built districts, and have left the houses, which were not good enough for them, to a population strongly mixed with Irish blood. Here one is in an almost undis-

guised working-men's quarter, for even the shops and beerhouses hardly take the trouble to exhibit a trifling degree of cleanliness. But all this is nothing in comparison with the courts and lanes which lie behind, to which access can be gained only through covered passages, in which no two human beings can pass at the same time. Of the irregular cramming together of dwellings in ways which defy all rational plan, of the tangle in which they are crowded literally one upon the other, it is impossible to convey an idea. And it is not the buildings surviving from the old times of Manchester which are to blame for this; the confusion has only recently reached its height when every scrap of space left by the old way of building has been filled up and patched over until not a foot of land is left to be further occupied.

. . .

Right and left a multitude of covered passages lead from the main street into numerous courts, and he who turns in thither gets into a filth and disgusting grime, the equal of which is not to be found – especially in the courts which lead down to the Irk, and which contain unqualifiedly the most horrible dwellings which I have yet beheld. In one of these courts there stands directly at the entrance, at the end of the covered passage, a privy without a door, so dirty that the inhabitants can pass into and out of the court only by passing through foul pools of stagnant urine and excrement. This is the first court on the Irk above Ducie Bridge – in case any one should care to look into it. Below it on the river there are several tanneries which fill the whole neighbourhood with the stench of animal putrefaction.

For a man of Engels's background and upbringing, a city meant a place in which life and work took place side by side. The new Manchester wasn't like that. The wealthy no longer lived above their counting rooms. It was as unfamiliar for a man who had lived in the medieval Hanseatic city of Bremen when young as the British architectural historian Reyner Banham would find Los Angeles a century later. The difference was that Engels was appalled by what he discovered in England, while Banham was determined to find something inspiring in Los Angeles, qualities that nobody else had yet seen.

In 1845, Manchester had fewer than 400,000 people. By the standards of the time, however, it was a giant city. The population was doubling and redoubling decade by decade. It was a city that seemed to represent a new model of urban life, where technical innovation coexisted with squalor, much as they still do in the backstreets of Shanghai. The rest of the world was fascinated and came to learn all that it could from Manchester's lessons as the emblematic city of the Industrial Revolution. As a result, there are industrial cities throughout the Americas named for Manchester, which also gave its name to an economic system based on free trade. The German architect Karl Friedrich Schinkel had been there 20 years before Engels, and deftly sketched the massive brick and iron mills of the Ancoats industrial area in an attempt to understand the techniques that were needed to build such unprecedented structures.

Manchester got under Engels's skin. It was a city that was the crystallization of all that he believed was wrong with the world; the most extreme, the most revealing, chaotic, dynamic, brutal artefact of its kind. And yet it was also the main driver of the capitalist system, which, as Marx and Engels saw it, was the essential precursor to the construction of the socialist order. Lenin ignored their belief that a transition from pre-capitalist feudalism to socialism which bypassed capitalism was impossible. Engels's account of the horrors of Manchester reflected the hostility many of his contemporaries had for all big cities.

Having invented the modern city in the wake of the Industrial

Revolution, many in Britain were overwhelmed by a sense of revulsion. William Morris, and others who thought like him, identified big cities with all that had gone wrong with the world. In 'Jerusalem', William Blake's savagely ironic verse of 1808, England's green and pleasant land had been overwhelmed by dark satanic mills that diminished the lives of the rural communities that flocked into the big cities to find work.

In his novel *News from Nowhere*, William Morris portrayed a London deserted after the fall of capitalism. Parliament Square is transformed into a dung heap, with worthless banknotes fluttering in the wind. The city's inhabitants have dispersed into the countryside to live the life of nineteenth-century hippies.

Although London had such modern innovations as street lighting and a suburban railway system, cholera became a deadly threat. The Thames was an open sewer responsible for the so-called 'Great Stink'; so noxious in its effects that parliamentarians in the hot summer of 1858 kept the windows of the newly completed Houses of Parliament tightly shut to keep out the smell. The stench was crippling, but the real danger, the accompanying cholera outbreaks, was only dealt with by Bazalgette's new sewers and pumping stations, built between 1865 and 1875. Even then, the Greenock-born German anarchist J. H. Mackay wrote in 1891: 'The East End of London is the hell of poverty. Like one enormous black, motionless giant kraken, the poverty of London lies there in lurking silence and encircles with its mighty tentacles the life and wealth of the City.'

It was the revulsion of nineteenth-century intellectuals against the city that made possible the attempts of Le Corbusier and his followers to use ruthless urban surgery to sanitize big cities in the twentieth century. Le Corbusier after all belonged to a generation for which the terror of the epidemics was still a vivid memory. It was not so long since cholera had been killing 20,000 Parisians a year.

The early moderns did all that they could to find ways of controlling the uncontrollable city. They understood it as a place in which a dark and malevolent hidden presence constantly threatened to break through the surface and engulf civilized values in an eruption of depravity, violence and squalor.

Aboard their chartered passenger ship the SS *Patris II*, the architects of the Congrès Internationaux d'Architecture Moderne (CIAM) set sail from Marseilles to Athens in the summer of 1933, to plot their strategy to tame the city. We do not belong to a generation that has the shared faith enjoyed by the pioneering architectural modernists. They divided their utopia into functional zones that segregated the home from the workplace. They believed that considerations of hygiene should be the primary factor determining the layout of social housing, which took the form of slabs set far enough apart in parkland to allow the sun to reach every corner of the space between them. Theirs was a generation free from the luxury of self-doubt. Ours is not, and that is why we struggle now in trying to find a renewed sense of purpose about what cities should be. We are the witnesses to the many soured urban utopias invented by the architects on that liner, bowdlerized and propagated by a political system that measured success by the number of new homes it could deliver each month. Apparently less violent, but equally destructive of urban values, was the growth of the garden city movement pioneered in the UK by Ebenezer Howard. But when it finally appeared, the dominant model for the low-density suburban city was not the teetotal, overgrown village that was the reality of Howard's garden city of Welwyn, but a sprawling monster called Los Angeles.

If Engels and Dickens explored the significance of the nineteenth-century industrial city with the written word, in the twentieth century it was film-makers who set out to predict what cities might become. And they were among the first to create a climate in which the darker, and apparently more sinister, aspects of urban life could be presented as a more sophisticated alternative to a sunny but antiseptic utopia.

Fritz Lang's *Metropolis* from 1927 laid the foundations for a tradition of cinema's exploration of urban dystopia that culminated in Ridley Scott's *Blade Runner* of 1982, by way of film noir such as Jules Dassin's *Night and the City*, made in 1950, which portrayed crime amid the bomb sites of post-war London as the Festival of Britain took shape out of the rubble.

Cinema has depicted the moral compromises and violence that have formed an apparently inevitable accompaniment to development. Francesco Rosi's *Hands over the City* made in 1963 portrayed Edoardo Nottola, played by Rod Steiger, as a ruthless property speculator who bends the law, intimidates, seduces and bribes politicians from every party to make his fortune from the reconstruction of Naples.

Anthony Minghella's 2006 film, *Breaking and Entering*, returns to the same slice of London that Dickens explored in *Dombey and Son* and provides an insightful exploration of the layered nature of the modern city. Jude Law is a landscape architect, busy making London safe for the world of upmarket noodle bars, lofts with sandblasted brick walls, and public art. The film is a nuanced critique of contemporary urbanism. It is a picture of two utterly different worlds that overlap in place but not in time. By day Law's studio, set in the midst of the vast redevelopment site that is King's Cross, hums with the comfortable sense of entitlement of middle-class creatives. At night it is overtaken by Nigerian cleaners and Kosovan crack dealers who keep coming back to steal his computers. Minghella's film is a reminder of how these two urban worlds depend on each other, but rarely see or speak to each other.

The conventional response of non-fictional planners is still to try to sweep the dark underbelly of the city away. They pacify *favelas*, and destroy the low-cost housing that makes life in the

Gustave Caillebotte depicted Parisian boulevard life (above).

George Tooker caught the alienation of mass transit in New York (top). Rod Steiger's Mafioso developer in *Hands over the City* (bottom) charts the shaping of a Naples trapped between ambition and profit.

The city is the key subject in art, literature and the cinema. Dickens and Zola captured the essence of London and Paris on the brink of modernization.

city possible for the poor, and, by accommodating service workers, more comfortable for the affluent.

If Manchester was the quintessential city of the first Industrial Revolution, a city of steam-powered looms, canals, telegraphs and trams, then Los Angeles represented the key city of consumerism, shaped first of all by the streetcar, then by the automobile. The image of the city was defined by the cinema, which made its landscape familiar all over the world. Oil wells and the beginnings of the aerospace industry made Los Angeles wealthy and ready to experiment with new ideas. It attracted a stream of displaced European intellectuals and artists, from Bertolt Brecht and Richard Neutra to Arnold Schoenberg and Thomas Mann.

With its photochemical smog and its endless sprawl, its tiers of concrete cloverleaf flyovers stacked two or three tiers high in some places, Los Angeles was regarded with almost as much horror as Manchester had once been, at least by those who did not live there. Then the British architectural historian Reyner Banham set out to change their minds. He said that he learned to drive at the age of 43 when he first arrived in the city so that, as he put it, he could read it in the original. Banham understood that Los Angeles was changing the world as much as Manchester had once done, but he was determined to celebrate the place, no matter how odious others found it. In fact, as his biographer Nigel Whiteley put it, Banham wanted to like Los Angeles precisely because other people didn't. The writer Adam Raphael, whom Banham gleefully quotes in his book, *Los Angeles: The Architecture of Four Ecologies*, suggested that 'Los Angeles is the noisiest, the smelliest, the most uncomfortable and the most uncivilized major city in the United States. In short a stinking sewer.'

James Cameron was more perceptive: it was a place, he wrote, of 'sinless joy and joyless sin'. Banham's 1971 book was an attempt at showing the polite world how to understand the city that they had previously regarded as the personification of all that could go wrong with urban life, overwhelmed by freeways, strip malls and junk architecture. In fact, Banham's book is not really about architecture; it has much more to do with offering a way of thinking about a city that previously had the ability to induce intense anxiety, even fear, in visitors. It could not have been written without Banham's association with the emergence of the Independent Group, the British forerunners of the pop art movement, and their fascination with the everyday and the allure of commercial popular culture.

Banham believed that LA's rotting downtown was irrelevant to the city as a whole. European visitors were left baffled and uncomprehending at streets without sidewalks where they could be stopped by the police for not owning a car. Where could you meet people? How did you get around when all the usual signs that they used to navigate a city had been eradicated? How did you tell a dangerous area from a safe one? The smog tinting blue skies a sinister brown, and intensifying already lurid sunsets, was also a new and particularly threatening phenomenon that seemed like an alien intrusion into what had once been the benign orange groves on which much of the city was built. When Banham arrived in 1964, Los Angeles seemed like the personification of placeless anonymity, a characteristic that was considered to be even worse in its effects than the pollution.

Gertrude Stein had her home town, Oakland in California, in mind when she suggested 'there is no there there', perhaps not to insult it but to describe the melancholy of revisiting the street that she had grown up on and no longer recognized. But in the 1960s the words were universally associated with what critics took to be the placelessness of Los Angeles and its lack of a centre. Banham believed that this was a response based on prejudice and a wilful inability to understand what Los Angeles had to offer.

In his permissive acceptance of the essence of Los Angeles, Banham was the prelude to the celebration of Las Vegas by

Robert Venturi and Denise Scott Brown, two architects with a good claim to be regarded as the first postmodernists. Later observers would come to Las Vegas for an insight into the new service economy and the jobs it created for Latino migrants to the USA, documented or not. Venturi and Scott Brown went to find a 'normal' city behind the explosion of the usually hidden desires revealed by the strip. What made *Learning from Las Vegas* different from previous explorations of the forces shaping contemporary cities was its at-the-time shocking determination to learn from popular culture.

> Visiting Las Vegas in the mid-1960s was like visiting Rome in the late 1940s. For young Americans in the 1940s, familiar only with the auto-scaled, gridiron city and the antiurban theories of the previous architectural generation, the traditional urban spaces, the pedestrian scale, and the mixtures, yet continuities, of styles of the Italian piazzas were a significant revelation. They rediscovered the piazza. Two decades later architects are perhaps ready for similar lessons about large open space, big scale, and high speed. Las Vegas is to the Strip what Rome is to the Piazza.

The novelist Mary McCarthy wrote an elegant little book about the impossibility of finding anything new to say about Venice. She could just as well have been talking about Las Vegas, a city that, since the Venturis went there with their students in the late 1960s, has been picked over by an even greater density of literary tourists, from Noël Coward to Hunter Thompson. Most of them identify the essentially industrial character of the place, in which the masses toil grim-faced around the clock on the production lines represented by the slot machines. Another regular observation is to point out the resemblance of Las Vegas to Lourdes: the terminally sick, the obese and the deformed journey here from all across the United States in search of redemption and the chance to touch, even if only for a fleeting instant, the dream of riches and gold on which the city is built. And yet, unlike Venice, Las Vegas is not dead: it continues to reinvent itself. It is, among other things, a stronghold of organized labour. The unions have ensured the city provides its waiting staff, its kitchen hands and its cleaners with a reasonable wage.

There was a time when the academically respectable slice of the architectural profession would have recoiled, like a vampire squirming away from sunshine, from being subjected to such an exercise in the kitschiest of kitsch. And yet Las Vegas occupies a special place in the history of contemporary architecture and urbanism. Venturi and Scott Brown claimed to address the divorce of contemporary architecture from popular culture; they attempted to do something about the nagging sense of intellectual insecurity at the heart of the architectural profession: the sense that architects simply didn't count in the wider world of culture, that they were regarded as concerned not with ideas but with the grubby pragmatism of construction.

Venturi and Scott Brown had declared that Las Vegas was not a tawdry freak show – the product of a bizarre shotgun marriage between organized crime and the New Deal, which financed the building of the Hoover Dam close by – but a contemporary Florence. They cruised the Strip, paced the car parks and surveyed the structure of what most architects, with the imagery of Tuscan hill towns indelibly marked on their minds, would not recognize as a city at all.

On the surface, 1960s Las Vegas was the very model of what not to do for an architectural profession still racked by a sense of mission predicated on the construction of a new social order. It was crassly, outrageously, tacky. And yet it was also the most vital source of visual imagery in the US. It had drive-in wedding chapels and enough winking neon to terrify the primmest of modern architects. The Venturis had the vision to swallow hard and decide that, actually, Las Vegas wasn't so bad. And they treated what they saw not with a tongue-in-cheek knowingness but with the utmost seriousness.

They saw strip development, with its giant illuminated signs, forecourt car parks and artless buildings, as a vernacular. It was, as they understood it, a landscape designed to be seen at the speed of a moving car rather than experienced by a pedestrian. To the Venturis, the Las Vegas vernacular was there to be quoted by academically trained architects and planners, and even translated into the basis of a literary form, while still retaining its accessibility to a wider audience. They might have been talking about the way in which John le Carré was able to transform the basic elements of the thriller into literature, or even what Warhol did with the imagery of commercial packaging. Rather than dream about the kind of city that architects could construct if only society would let them, the Venturis were more interested in the world as it was. 'Many people like suburbia, this is the reason for learning from Levittown and Las Vegas . . . We must go to the suburban edges of the existing city that are symbolically rather than formalistically attractive.' But the messy vitality of the Las Vegas that inspired them was already on the way out, to be replaced first by vacuum-formed, backlit Perspex, then by LEDs, just as Burger King has replaced the diner. For all its apparent radicalism, *Learning from Las Vegas* is full of nostalgia for redundant technology. The Las Vegas of the Venturis was no more the authentic Las Vegas than Jane Jacobs's nostalgic view of the gentle street life of Greenwich Village was the real New York.

The Venturis would not recognize present-day Las Vegas. Glitter Gulch, where the workers who built the Hoover Dam came on payday to stuff their money into the slot machines, could not keep up with the new casinos. The city announces itself now, not with pop art cowboys, but with hotel restaurants that serve $4,000 bottles of wine and display Picassos from the collection of casino owner Steve Wynn. If the Las Vegas of the 1960s helped fuel Andy Warhol, today's city is more in the manner of Jeff Koons. Las Vegas's unique contribution to contemporary architecture and urbanism has its roots in the landscaped grounds of the eighteenth-century English country houses, with their classical follies and Gothic grottoes that in turn recall the way in which the Emperor Hadrian evoked the Nile and its monuments in his villa outside Rome. In the course of two decades, the rival casino owners kept raising the stakes in their competition with each other to create the most flamboyant Las Vegas landmarks. They have to do more than just attract traffic cruising west along the Strip.

The casinos, having pulled the crowds into the middle of the desert, have to offer things to do, as well as things to look at. Like a triple cheeseburger with all the trimmings and a side order of fries, in the constant competition to outdo each other, the casinos merge layer upon layer of ingredients: gambling with boxing, music with circus, shopping with eating with theme park, convention centre with Guggenheim museum, in some cases all in the same complex. It has given the centre of Las Vegas the form of a roulette wheel on which the owners place bets on several different properties at the same time, in the hope of spreading their risks.

At one end is the MGM Grand, a hulking green monster, with its trademark lion pumped up 10 storeys high. And at 5,000 rooms, not so much one of the world's largest hotels as a fair-sized town.

On the adjacent corner is the Excalibur, a little smaller than the MGM Grand, but no less conspicuous. An animatronic dragon clambers out of its moat at regular intervals in a vigorous but futile effort to swallow a wizard. The Tropicana's clump of larger-than-life Easter Island heads stakes its claim to attention. It faces the Excalibur, which in turn confronts the MGM. And the MGM's lion glowers across multiple lanes of traffic at the Statue of Liberty erupting from a lake traversed by the Brooklyn

Bridge that takes guests to the Hotel New York New York, which is fashioned from a clump of replica Manhattan skyscrapers at 1/3 scale. Inside, the 80,000-square-foot casino is themed on Central Park. The auditorium is Radio City. And there is a rollercoaster ride with a 200-foot drop in which customers sit in approximations of yellow cabs. It is a hallucination of a hallucination.

New York New York found itself upstaged by the Venetian, with its replica of St Mark's Square, its gondolas, canals and bridges, and its shortlived outpost of the Guggenheim in a rusty Corten steel box designed by Rem Koolhaas. The Venetian, with its campaniles and its representation of the Doge's Palace, brings higher standards of craftsmanship to the project than New York New York could manage, where the idea of replicating the spiral of the original Guggenheim was supposedly dropped in favour of a representation of the less geometrically demanding and so cheaper, Whitney Museum.

At the start of the twenty-first century, this was the style that escaped from the theme park and went on the rampage like hogweed: its effects are visible in every shopping centre dressed up to look like a village green, and every airport with a hipster bar with mid-century modern salvaged chairs in the departure lounge. And in Las Vegas, MGM Resorts started the CityCenter project on the Strip, which brings together high-profile architects, including Norman Foster, and a mix of elements that goes beyond casinos and hotel units to include 2,400 apartments, as well as street-level retail, and a mass transit system, as if Las Vegas has started to become a little more like a real city. Venturi and Scott Brown suggested that rather than rush to judgement, it was more important to understand what was going on in this new form of the city.

> Learning from the existing landscape is a way of being revolutionary for an architect. Not the obvious way, which is to

> tear down Paris and begin again, as Le Corbusier wanted to in the 1920s, but another, more tolerant way; that is, to question how we look at things.
>
> [. . .] The Las Vegas Strip in particular [. . .] challenges the architect to take a positive, non-chip-on-the-shoulder view. [. . .]
>
> And withholding judgment may be used as a tool to make later judgement more sensitive. This is a way of learning from everything.

This is exactly what Banham did with Los Angeles, and what the Dutch architect and theorist Rem Koolhaas would go on to do with his as yet unpublished study of Lagos, already 20 years in the writing. Koolhaas's first book, *Delirious New York*, published in 1978, suggested that by decoding what he presented as the real meanings of Manhattan's urban history he offered the possibility of coming to an understanding of the history of twentieth-century cities – 'a retrospective manifesto', he called it. Koolhaas's firm, OMA, went on to work on many of the most emblematic projects of the world's emerging cities. They built China Central TV's Beijing headquarters, and a series of cultural projects in Qatar. Focusing on Lagos, a city unfamiliar to the perpetually jet-lagged troupe of internationally successful architects that circle the world building museums and skyscrapers, was attractive precisely because it was a less obvious choice.

Banham and Koolhaas take a wilfully contrarian view. They have both explored cities in which received wisdom told them that they were not meant to find many redeeming features. But rather than condemn, they present them as, if not a model of urbanity, then at least an object worth taking seriously. Koolhaas first went to Lagos in 1996, and has been promising to publish his book entitled *Lagos: How it Works* for several years. It exists in the public world only as an unfulfilled promise on an Amazon

For centuries our understanding of cities was shaped, if not always by the traditional European models of Rome and Florence, Paris and Vienna, London and Berlin, then by the conventional historical examples: Beijing or Athens. In the second half of the twentieth century, a new generation of observers established their own reputations by looking at shockingly different models of the city. Reyner Banham explored Los Angeles (above), Robert Venturi and Denise Scott Brown went to Las Vegas, and Rem Koolhaas discovered Lagos.

Designed to be understood at the pace of the car, Las Vegas is still a place in which people walk in the streets between the architectural set pieces and where the poor are drawn to try to touch the aura of wealth, like limbless pilgrims to Santiago de Compostella looking for sanctity.

Of all Africa's cities, Lagos is the one that stands out for its sheer scale, and its capacity to function in the midst of apparent chaos.

page with a fictitious publication date of 2007. There is however, a film, *Lagos Wide & Close*, on which Koolhaas collaborated. In it, he suggests: 'What is now fascinating is how with some level of self-organization there is a strange combination of extreme underdevelopment and development . . . [Lagos is] not a kind of backward situation but an announcement of the future.'

Koolhaas describes a city that has many aspects Engels would recognize from his experience of Manchester in the 1840s. But, unlike Engels, who, from the tone of his impatience with what he describes as the disorder of Manchester's haphazard growth would probably have been happy to see its existing form wiped out and replaced with something more disciplined, Koolhaas resolutely claims to find, if not pleasure, then life, and lessons about life, in Lagos. 'Sometimes you don't know how afraid you have to be because the stories of violence and robberies are so extreme. Lagos has the most horrible reputation in terms of safety, but it can be exciting to face fears and stare them down.'

Koolhaas describes an evening in a Lagos nightclub, which got him in the cross hairs of those critics who see him as a self-indulgent disaster tourist, able to fetishize the slum but be helicoptered out in case of real trouble. 'It was totally unclear where we were, because it was pitch dark, and there had been no electricity for many hours before we arrived. So for the first time in my life I was eating – in pitch dark – food that I could not see or identify.'

Undaunted, Koolhaas proceeded to construct a view of what Africa's largest metropolis, the focus of a state that is overtaking South Africa and Johannesburg as the urban epicentre of the continent, looks like.

> In Lagos there is no choice, but there are countless ways to articulate the condition of no choice. In New York, on the other hand, there's a sense of infinite choice, but a very conventional set of options from which to choose. I've never

been particularly interested in the individual inhabitant of the city, but in Lagos there was a fantastic levelling. We became so familiar with the city that we ceased to maintain our objective approach, and actually entered the field. From these more vulnerable positions, we could feel the impact of all forces.

...

[Lagos] was frightening and shocking, not depressing. Of course its extremely depressing if you think about the quality of life. But I've seen so many positive forces there that I never actually got depressed . . . Whatever doubts you might have about Lagos, it at least offers a perspective that many cultures didn't have even 10 or 20 years ago.

In Los Angeles, Banham found a 'city seventy miles square, but rarely seventy years deep apart from a small downtown not yet two centuries old and a few other pockets of ancientry, Los Angeles is instant architecture in an instant townscape'. Banham was intoxicated by customized dragsters and surfboards, and the social tics of freeway etiquette that he claimed to have observed, such as the fixing of hair in the passenger mirrors of cars by their occupants as they came off the freeways and which he interpreted as marking the transition from outdoors to indoors. For Banham, San Francisco was just too much like what he already knew in Europe to be interesting.

San Francisco was plugged into California from the sea; the Gold Rush brought its first population and their culture round Cape Horn; their prefabricated Yankee houses and prefabricated New England (or European) attitudes were dumped unmodified on the Coast. Viewed from Southern California it looks like a foreign enclave, like the Protestant Pale in Ireland, because the Southern Californians came, predominantly, overland to Los Angeles, slowly traversing the whole North American land-mass and its evolving history.

Banham was a provocative observer who played an important part in shaping the way that we understand the contemporary city. He helped us look at cities without preconceptions, to find the positive aspects of the unfamiliar. But he missed a phenomenon that was already underway at the other end of California from Los Angeles, on the outer edge of San Francisco. If there is anywhere that can be seen as the ground zero of what has become the world's dominant industry, it is Silicon Valley. The place is, of course, a figure of speech, rather than an actual city with a government and a tax base. Nevertheless, it describes a place that has had an impact on the world's culture and its economy to match that of any city in the last 50 years. It has attracted the talented and the ambitious from around the world; it has created new forms of workplace, new patterns of commuting, and it has accelerated the rate of change. Beyond the two freeways that form a long, thin rectangle between San Francisco and San Jose is a string of little towns which constitute Silicon Valley and which barely existed in the 1950s. This can be understood as a city not because of its manufacturing capacity (the chip factories are elsewhere), nor for its size or form of government, but because of the people that it is able to attract, a factor that became self-reinforcing when the first generation of computer companies emerged from their garages. Apple, Google and Facebook are all here. Uber and Airbnb, who are transforming transport and hotelkeeping in cities respectively, are not far away, along with LinkedIn and Twitter. The world has come to look and learn, just as the world went to explore England's industrial cities at the start of the nineteenth century.

If Silicon Valley has a centre, it is Stanford University – actually

Leland Stanford Junior University, named in 1885, in memory of their only son, who died in childhood, by his grieving parents, Governor Leland Stanford and his wife, Jane. And close by, on Sand Hill Road in Menlo Park, is its financial centre, where the venture capital funds cluster together. Stanford was built on the 8,000 acres of farmland that the family donated to the university. Frederick Law Olmsted laid out the campus, and it developed in a uniform mission style, with sandstone walls and red roof tiles.

Stanford now has 30,000 students and staff, 14 square miles of nature reserves served by a ring road, called Campus Drive, connecting it to the two freeways that are the main arteries of Silicon Valley. In addition to the nature reserves, it has a golf course and its own particle accelerator. William Hewlett and David Packard, Stanford graduates in the 1930s, were the first to start a high-tech business in a garage in Palo Alto. Yahoo, Sun Microsystems, Netflix, LinkedIn, eBay and a score of other successful enterprises are linked to the university. Larry Page and Sergey Brin did the early work that made Google possible on campus and gave the university shares in the new company to license the intellectual property. It is the kind of institution that every ambitious city in the world would like to replicate. When he was Mayor of New York, Michael Bloomberg tried to persuade Stanford to set up a second campus on Governors Island in the middle of the East River. In Britain, Cambridge comes closest to Stanford's remarkable record in turning out graduates who have put their academic training to use to start businesses that have achieved worldwide dominance apparently instantaneously.

The university's presence has made Northern California home to some of the world's richest corporations, and they in turn have made the university wealthy. Apple, which reached a market capitalization of $710 billion in 2015, making it worth more than the GDPs of Switzerland, Nigeria and Poland, among many other nations, is based in Cupertino. Google is in Mountain View. On a good day, getting to Google by car from One Infinite Loop, as Apple's present headquarters calls itself, takes just six minutes. Google knows more about us than the US National Security Agency (NSA) and the UK Government Communications Headquarters (GCHQ). It will soon start selling self-driving cars and is working on contact lenses that can monitor blood sugar levels for diabetics. Google can tell us exactly how long a drive will take before we have even started. Menlo Park, another 16 minutes on US 101 heading westward, is home to Facebook, which has more people logging on each day – which is to say, using its products – than the entire population of China.

Apple, Facebook, Google and, up in Seattle, Amazon, are each city states, with no democratic pretensions. They are oligarchies that famously feel no obligation to pay taxes. For Italy's city states, there used to be some sort of checks and balances, between civic and religious authority, between pope and emperor. In Silicon Valley, there are no balances. It is the home of a cluster of global superpowers, the product of vertiginous growth, answerable only to themselves, and yet they depend on the wider city region of which they are part, just as Florence and Siena depended on the wider Italian context for their culture, identity and security. And they threaten to overshadow the state, even if enlightened self-interest might suggest otherwise.

The total population of the Bay Area is scattered across eight counties and amounts to around seven million people. This is the kind of urban soup that I once described as *The 100 Mile City*, where pockets of traditional urbanism float in among open country, sprawling business parks and vast transport depots. It has within it one or two components that would be recognized as cities by European standards. San Francisco, with about 900,000 people within the city limits, is the most densely populated city in America. It has a downtown and it has pedestrian life, as well as one of America's most visible groups of homeless people. A long stretch of Mission Street with its flophouses and street sleepers is precisely the area where tech start-ups have been looking for space for their offices. San Francisco is full of the things that are conventionally associated with urban life: pavements, pedestrians, bookshops, an opera house, Chinese street food and public transport.

Oakland, with rather fewer inhabitants, is similar. San Jose looks a lot less like a traditional city, as it is green, low rise and low density, but after decades of steadily expanding its borders it claims to have more people within its jurisdiction than San Francisco.

If people work in Silicon Valley, they do not necessarily live there. Commuter buses taking Google programmers out to Mountain View have come under attack from the more radical of San Franciscans. And the money made in Silicon Valley has had a big impact on property values in San Francisco's residential streets. Over the past six decades, Silicon Valley has been through successive iterations, the first of which was the research phase, when Xerox shipped over some of its best brains from the freezing winters of upstate New York to Palo Alto. They were accommodated in the purpose-built Palo Alto Research Center, Xerox PARC. This is where the early work was done on what would become the graphical user interface (or GUI) that opened up computing to the wider world when it was commercialized by Steve Jobs.

Xerox's scientists and the early technology companies found themselves sharing Northern California with hippies and Stewart Brand's *Whole Earth Catalog* types. Brand was a key figure in the crossover between the worlds of technology and the counterculture that was to inform Steve Jobs and later Sergey Brin and Larry Page at Google. He once lived on a boat moored in Sausalito, just across the Golden Gate Bridge from San Francisco. Tom Wolfe's *Electric Kool-Aid Acid Test* non-fictional account of Ken Kesey's

LSD-fuelled road trip in search of the Grateful Dead, Hells Angels and Timothy Leary portrays Brand at the wheel of the magic bus full of Merry Pranksters. He published *The Whole Earth Catalog*; it was an analogue ancestor of Wikipedia, and carried the subtitle 'access to tools', which went from solar panels to geodesic domes, emerging VCR technologies and self-sufficiency. The 1969 edition had a cover image of Earth as a blue disc in swirling cloud in stark contrast to the deep black void of space. Here was Buckminster Fuller's Spaceship Earth, brought to life.

Brand played an important role working with Douglas Engelbart, the engineer credited with the invention of the computer mouse, hypertext and email. In 1968, Engelbart demonstrated the potential of all of these new tools at an event that he called 'The Mother of All Demos', where Brand was operating a remote camera. This cross-fertilization between utopian speculation, physics and mathematics, and between self-reliant autonomy and wealth creation is what has shaped the urbanism of Silicon Valley. It is a view of city life that is based on a mix of the utopian and the brutally unsentimental, in which the pace of change is continually accelerating, in which all apparently public space is private under the watchful gaze of constantly swivelling surveillance, and where the corporation has commandeered the individual employee's life and leisure with constant connectedness and the Apple watch has become a symbol of servitude. Three of the four most powerful and richest corporations on the planet are building themselves prodigious new headquarters in the area that we pay as much attention as Engels and Schinkel gave to Manchester and its mills.

Steve Jobs made one of his last public appearances in Cupertino's community centre. Cupertino wants no more offices, and has a blanket 45-foot-height limit on new developments. It had declared itself full. But Jobs got his way when he presented his plan for a new HQ for Apple in 2011. Norman Foster, in close dialogue with Jobs, and then after Jobs's death with Apple's best-known designer,

Jony Ive, gave the building the form of a continuous ring. It will accommodate 16,000 people when it is completed.

If scale is one aspect of the Silicon city state, rapid change is another. By local standards Apple is a mature, long-established business. It has been in Cupertino since the earliest days, when it emerged from the garage in which Jobs and Steve Wozniak first started thinking about computers in 1976. But in the six years between 2009 and 2015, Facebook has grown even more rapidly than Apple and occupied four different headquarter buildings. It moved from an office in Palo Alto to a building on the Stanford science park; and from the science park it acquired what had been the one million square feet that Sun Microsystems had built for itself in Menlo Park, big enough for the 6,000 staff it was employing by 2012. And then Zuckerberg asked Frank Gehry to put as many of his staff as possible in a single space. It is a measure of the speed of change in Silicon Valley that industrial empires, which would once have taken several lifetimes to build, now explode and crumple there as quickly as a smartphone becomes obsolete.

Like Google, Sun Microsystems had been started by a couple of Stanford graduate students in 1982. It had 38,000 employees around the world by 2006. Four years later it had vanished. Zuckerberg bought the building when the company was sold to Oracle in 2010. Zuckerberg's designers from a firm called Gensler treated a building that had won awards for its environmental efficiency when it was completed in 1996 as if it were an industrial dinosaur from the steam age. The driving principle for Zuckerberg was to have people work together in unplanned random interactions. Sun had organized their building around what it called an 'internal street'. It's the same metaphor that the Gensler team brought to the project. But Zuckerberg's staff moved into a building that looked as if it had been occupied by upmarket squatters: there is graffiti art, installations, recycled furniture, and the annoyingly teenaged message 'Move Fast and Break

Silicon Valley, with its origins in the Stanford campus (top), is already old enough to have moved through a series of incarnations. The first golden age of garage start-ups gave way to pastel-coloured business parks. Now we are in the era of monument building by the giants – Facebook (above), Apple (opposite, top) and Google (opposite).

Things' on the slogan-filled walls. By contrast, when IBM was in its pomp in the 1960s, walls were filled with Paul Rand's elegantly crafted suggestions that demanded 'THINK!'

Facebook has moved beyond its retro-fitted home in what was once Sun Microsystems's building in Menlo Park into a sprawling studio space designed by Frank Gehry that allows Zuckerberg to sit in the middle of what looks like the largest room in the world, surrounded by 2,800 of his employees.

Google, based over in Mountain View, has considered a variety of expansion plans, first with what would once have been the obvious mainstream firm of NBBJ, who specialized in American corporate architecture, and more recently with the unstable pairing of the hyperactive Danish architect Bjarke Ingels and British designer Thomas Heatherwick.

While Cupertino gave Apple permission to build its new HQ, Mountain View took a tougher line. It did not want to see itself turning into a single-company town. The Ingels/Heatherwick project was for a notional two million square feet. In consciously unconventional blue-sky thinking, robots that were 'hackable' – the new word for adaptable – would be used to create endlessly flexible customizable layouts. Google employees would work under artificial skies, giant bubbles that suggested lessons had been learned from Buckminster Fuller's geodesic domes. But Mountain View said that it would consent to only 25 per cent of the scheme, and wanted to see LinkedIn take the rest of the space.

These are places that recall the scale of the huge ex-urban complexes of the East Coast that housed the bureaucrats who left New York for the suburbs. But the Silicon Valley behemoths are not cast in the traditional model of buttoned-down business cubicles. These are not offices or call centres, they are hothouses for creative minds. They are filled with brains that need careful nurturing. Those brains belong, mostly, to the young and the narcissistic. They demand in-house cycle repair shops to get their

Pinarello fixed. They need beanbags and pizza windows; they need in-house resident artists. They need vegan food and tofu. They need to be able to interact with each other like crazy, all the time.

The American writer Alexandra Lange compares the Foster building for Apple unfavourably with the other Silicon Valley giants' plans. She sees it as looking back to the days when the big corporations like Union Carbide moved out of Manhattan and into purpose-built office complexes in lush suburban Connecticut, and, shortly after, expired of boredom and irrelevance. But those East Coast offices from the 1960s made a clear distinction between work and leisure, between the company's time and that of the individual. Facebook and Google attempt to recreate the casual informality of fashionable street life within the compound of a security-controlled environment. They are, in a sense, infantilizing their workforces. In their working lives, they remain in a semi-permanent state of adolescence; the Facebook HQ is like a college town, without any dorms. In contrast, Foster's highly polished structure, which is inevitably compared to the industrial design of the company's products, seems to treat its employees as adults. They are working, not in a Starbucks or the lobby of the Ace Hotel, but in a grown-up building, dedicated to research and creative thinking.

We do not yet know the likely lifespan of the town-sized complexes that Silicon Valley is building. They could vanish even more rapidly than Sun Microsystems. But the big companies now have unprecedented economic power in very few hands. This is a place which saw Kodak, with its massive revenues for so many decades and its 80,000 skilled jobs, vanish. Nobody in Silicon Valley has any intention of going the same way.

The usual claim about the Silicon Valley complexes is that they turn their back on the city, and then try to inject the essence of city life into their controlled environments. Over the years they have got better and better at creating the signals that suggest authentic urbanism in the contexts in which they operate. It's the Disney version of urbanism, which over the years has gone from ersatz substitute for the original to supplanting it. The question that has yet to be answered is whether they will be any better at encouraging the kind of corporate culture that will help them escape the same fate as Kodak.

The old Apple complex in Cupertino carries the unmistakable flavour of the vanilla-coloured blocks of a generic high-tech business park, lost in the endless parking lots that characterize the workplaces of Northern California. They are the appropriately bland expression of the kind of lurking, mildly sinister, late capitalism that could have come from the pages of a J. G. Ballard novel: a world corralled behind invisible fences, constantly swept by gyrating security cameras; a world that has apparently turned its back on the complexities and the random accidents of city life. Foster's building will be something altogether more ambitious, and different in its scale and its purpose It offers the possibility of a piece of a city that might even outlive the corporation that built it.

It is missing something to see Silicon Valley as a place with no past. As long ago as three quarters of a century before Jobs established himself here, it was already attracting remarkable individuals from around the world. Camillo Olivetti, a bright graduate student from Italy was at Stanford before he went home to start his own company a century before Google existed. In the early days, Olivetti's company made typewriters, then it went on to mechanical calculating machines, and then, in 1959, under the guidance of Camillo's son, Adriano, Olivetti built Italy's first mainframe computer.

It is instructive to compare how Olivetti – for decades seen, much like Apple, as the most admired design-led corporation in the world – housed their research teams with the way that Apple does the job. Olivetti's designers were based not in Ivrea, the company town on the edge of Turin (not so different from Cupertino or Mountain View), but on the Corso Venezia in the heart of Milan. They believed it was the only way to attract people of the calibre that they needed. They were housed in a honey-coloured stone seminary built in the baroque style in 1652 by Francesco Maria Richini. The entrance had an elaborate pediment and cornice, a rusticated base and was flanked by a pair of caryatids. Across the courtyard there was still a chapel on the ground floor of the old seminary building; the archdiocese rented out the upper two floors to the company. Olivetti has long gone, but Corso Venezia is still a handsome and vital piece of the city 30 years later.

The Silicon Valley model of urbanism has yet to prove its longevity. Until now it has evolved by tearing down what has gone before. It has built an alternative economic model of urbanism that is the very opposite of the Manchester of the nineteenth century. It has no need of an industrial proletariat – having outsourced it to Asia. The elite are tended to by barmen and chefs, cleaners and chauffeurs, yoga instructors, bankers and lawyers. Silicon Valley is a city that has no need of high-rise office towers, factories or blue-collar suburbs.

It is an economy that is based on an unprecedented embrace of speed and change. For the first time in history, new products can sell in their millions over the launch weekend. It is a speed of change that leaves no time for monuments.

But just as the digital explosion has not ended the human need for physical, material objects, from the cult of vinyl records, to books and art, so Silicon Valley leaves a hunger for a more permanent form of city-building, one that leaves the traces of life lived in it, and time passing.

Chapter Six

Crowds and Their Discontents

A city without people is a dead city. The crowd is the essential sign of city life. A living city is the embodiment of the people who inhabit it. They fill its streets and its public spaces; they pour in every day to find all that a city has to offer.

Crowds come to work or to study. They come to a city to be healed or to be entertained. A city can provide solace and companionship. Some, in the crowds that a city generates, use it as a place to transgress in the pursuit of pleasure or profit. Others use the crowd as an escape from isolation, or the sense of their own insignificance. A crowd is as unstable, unpredictable and as volatile as the city itself. As the horrific stampede that killed perhaps 2,000 people in Mecca during the haj pilgrimage of 2015 tragically demonstrated, it can turn from an entity experiencing a shared religious duty into panic in an instant, or, as in the organization that every fifteen years creates the instant city of 50 million that is Kumbh Mele, the Hindu Ceremony on the Ganges, it can be an assertion of human organization.

Without warning, crowds can become unreasoning mobs, like those that attacked Tokyo's ethnic Korean citizens in the murderous pogroms that followed the earthquake of 1923, in the misplaced belief that they were responsible for the fires that consumed the city. London's Gordon Riots of the summer of 1780 saw the British army shoot dead 285 people after crowds, who had peacefully petitioned the House of Commons, turned into mobs that burned jails, freed prisoners, destroyed Catholic houses and churches and looted the property of the affluent without sectarian discrimination. Two hundred years later, 900 people were killed in 1992 in Mumbai, when Hindu mobs went on the rampage after Muslim protests against the destruction of a sixteenth-century mosque. They died in the confined spaces of the slums for much the same reasons that have caused so many deaths from mob violence over the years – a mix of wickedness, visceral fear and hate.

Yet crowds can also counterbalance a police force that is out of control, as happened in Los Angeles, with the attack on Rodney

King or Michael Brown's death in Ferguson. They can provide the witness that discourages official wrongdoing. It takes a crowd to demand the right of collective bargaining from an unreasonable employer. Crowds can bring down governments, as they did in Cairo's Tahrir Square in 2011. Crowds can mourn the death of a princess in a car crash, celebrate a football triumph, or mark the end of a war more with relief than the elation that is expected to accompany military victory.

A city without crowds is in the grip of fear of one kind or another. In Leptis Magna, the ancient Roman port city on the Libyan coast that has been deserted since the seventh century, the deep grooves cut into the stone walls of the harbour jetty by the cables that had once held grain ships in place as they loaded up for the journey across the Mediterranean to the Roman port of Ostia 2,000 years ago are still visible. The stone benches on the lip of the amphitheatre have views beyond the stage out to sea. Rows of Medusa masks ring the forum. Once it was possible to wander through streets of wine shops and bathhouses, reflecting on the multiple tragedies and rebirths that have taken place here over so many centuries. Now, you could reflect on the message that an empty Leptis sends us about the future of our own cities. The desolation and emptiness of a dead city can offer the melancholy dignity of a memento mori. The collapse of all central authority in Libya makes it too dangerous to visit Leptis now, and the city is in the midst of the kind of fear that does not permit reflection. It doesn't take the imposition of an official curfew – the most anti-urban act conceivable short of the physical destruction of a city or its people – to empty its streets. Fear is enough to do the job.

We are afraid of how cities change in ways that take away our memories of who we, and those who came before us, once were. We are afraid of growing old and poor alone. So, in certain circumstances, panic can cause the streets of a city to fill, but the presence of people is almost always a more positive sign than a negative one.

A street full of life suggests that a city is in good shape, that fear of actual or perceived threats is outweighed by the optimistic sense of potential that a city offers. We fear crime, sickness and terror. We fear the crowd, and the crowd fears itself. We are afraid of others in the city who are not like us. We are afraid not just that they will do us physical harm, but that they will change the way in which we live our lives. We are afraid of losing ourselves, we are afraid of betraying ourselves, and revealing that we do not belong.

Without the possibility of a crowd, a city is incomplete. There are few streets and fewer crowds in Silicon Valley. That is why, when the Giants win the World Series, San Francisco's Market Street fills up with people who have driven in to celebrate from across the whole Bay Area. They need to feel part of a crowd for the sense of shared experience that it brings. And it is this craving that may account for the remarkable phenomenon of the Indianapolis Speedway. In the midst of a flat, empty landscape dotted here and there with small towns and villages, the track has 250,000 seats for spectators for its car races, and can take up to 400,000 people – a figure to compare with the 850,000 people who live in Indianapolis itself, six miles away. On race days, it delivers a taste of the crowd for those who have no chance of experiencing it in any other way.

When the crowd takes over a city, ignoring it is no longer an option. Either you identify with it, or you try to hide from it. The crowd becomes a physical experience, in which the spatial form of the city plays a significant part. Equally, the principles that shape the movement of crowds through those spaces can begin to take on the characteristics of fluid dynamics. The freedom of action of the individual is curtailed by the press of bodies and the constrictions of space.

Congested streets full of people become a crowd only when those people become self-aware. But the impact of large numbers of people in a city is felt not just in the form of self-aware crowds.

Chapter Six

The crowd is the expression both of democratic energy and of mindless threat. Tahrir Square in Cairo (above) went from a forum for revolutionary change to a killing ground by an out-of-control police force and a misogynistic mob.

New Year in Cologne in 2016, when tensions between migrants and the German host community surfaced, as outrage over a wave of sexual assaults carried out under the cover of celebrating crowds spilled over.

Chapter Six

Through the sheer weight of numbers, tourism is threatening not just the character of some cities but their physical fabric too. Using padlocks as tokens of love is an instant tradition that began as a charming gesture, and has come to threaten the structural integrity of some Parisian bridges.

The Louvre now has to deal with 10 million visitors a year. The most popular attractions, stalked by visitors like African big game – the *Venus de milo*, *Winged Victory*, and, here, the *Mona Lisa* – are overwhelmed by crowds ten-deep taking selfies.

The streets of the world's biggest cities are permanently filled with people, in some places at almost all times of day or night. It's a reflection partly of the steady increase in the world's population in absolute numbers, and also of the increasing mobility of more and more people.

London overtook Paris to become Europe's most popular tourist city in 2014. It attracted 16.8 million overseas tourists who stayed for one night or more. That number has grown by more than eight million in a decade, and is now ahead of the 15.2 million overseas visitors that Paris attracted in the same year. For London that means there are two visitors for every permanent resident. Those visitors are not all here at the same time, so the pressure of numbers is spread throughout the year, but it could be seen to add a significant increase to London's population at any given moment. And those people are not evenly distributed throughout the city: they concentrate in just a few precisely delineated areas on which their presence has an overwhelming impact. Such places include the gateways to a city. In 2014, Heathrow Airport, now no longer the world's busiest in terms of international flights, recorded 73.4 million passengers taking off or landing.

On one level, the fact that so many people can pass through a confined space, and be reunited with their luggage at the end of the process, is a triumph of organization and planning. When the Victorians built railways stations they had great difficulty with the massive crowds that flocked to them on holidays as traffic grew, and were continually having to rebuild and reorder them.

Some airports are better than others at handling numbers of people that would be extraordinary in any circumstance, had we not become so accustomed to them. But the layout of an airport, and its relationship with the city that it serves, has become one of the key aspects of urban design in the twenty-first century. To accommodate all the people who are attracted to the most visited cities of the world, we are normalizing gatherings of unprecedentedly vast numbers. Airports are being planned now that can deal with 450,000 passengers moving through them in the course of a single day. That will be like moving the entire adult population of Edinburgh every day, with an aircraft landing each minute for a full 24 hours.

Airports have a chance of going back to first principles and being re-engineered with the ruthlessness that Hong Kong showed when its original airport, Kai Tak, was replaced with an entirely new one, involving reclaiming land from the sea for the runways and terminals, and building new roads, bridges and railways to get passengers there. But the historic cores of Europe's great cities are not so easily adapted. In each of them is a tightly defined landscape, made up of the 10 or 20 places at which visitors pause to take photographs.

These are the very restricted numbers of landmarks that serve to define a visit to a city. Such places were rarely designed for dense concentrations of people, and their character is now being eroded by the pressure of growing crowds. Tourists move in ever larger herds. First it was Venice, with its permanent population down to less than 35,000, that was seen as the victim of a tragic hollowing out, the transformation of the husk of what was once one of the world's great cultural, financial and political powers into a glum pedestrian circuit, with no room or time to pause on the bridges. The same phenomenon is threatening other cities. It is overwhelming the steps serving London's Tower Bridge, built for a trickle of nineteenth-century pedestrians, now used by tens of thousands, wearing down the granite treads. Some bridges over the Seine on which visitors leave their padlocks, throwing the keys into the river, eventually became so encrusted with excess metal that they were threatened with structural damage. Huge numbers of visitors come to London and Paris, and almost all of them want to visit just a few places, led by the kind of guides who deploy small flags or umbrellas to keep their charges in sight, and who use portable loudspeakers to amuse their listeners. This is a new, and accelerating, phenomenon. In 2012, a staggering 9.7 million people found their way through the four main entrances of the Louvre. On a particularly busy day those visitors unwise enough to choose to attempt to enter through I. M. Pei's Pyramid and the Cour Napoléon could find themselves waiting for two or more hours as they negotiated successive bottlenecks. First they snaked around the Louvre's courtyard in the rain. Then they had to wait again to buy a ticket; and for a third time if they wanted to leave their coats and umbrellas.

When François Mitterrand commissioned I. M. Pei in the 1980s to remodel the Louvre by inserting a glass pyramid into the heart of the museum's central courtyard, the idea was to help first-time visitors make more sense of the sprawling institution and its apparently endless galleries. It was a scheme designed to deal with what seemed at the time to be an unimaginable 4.5 million visitors each year. Now, after negotiating the bag checks and the ticket counters, the 9.7 million visitors find themselves standing 10 deep in front of the *Mona Lisa*, complaining bitterly to TripAdvisor and each other about the selfish behaviour of their neighbours. They accuse them of elbowing their way to the front to picture themselves with one of the Big Three: the familiar sequence of the *Venus de Milo*, the *Winged Victory of Samothrace* and the *Mona Lisa*.

Why, some complain, could they not all be kept in the same room, to make it easier for those in a hurry to get in and out, having seen all that they wanted to? In this view of the world the *Mona Lisa* is Paris, just as *The Night Watch* is Amsterdam and the Kremlin is Moscow. As the Louvre is threatened with being overwhelmed by a doubling in the number of its visitors, the museum has set out on yet another remodelling. It is investing €50 million in a new design that is intended to cut down those queues and apply some of the lessons learned from airport methods for handling large numbers of people. London's British Museum has suffered from the same phenomenon. When it first opened in the eighteenth century, offering free admission to the studious and the curious, around 5,000 people came in a year. The annual total has reached 6.7 million, with the busiest single day recently seeing just under 34,000 people pouring through the building. Since the British Museum does not charge admission, this is a slightly less frustrating experience than negotiating the tills at the Louvre.

Population growth is making us adjust cities to the demands of crowds. Bigger cities, with more visitors as well as more residents, need larger and larger spaces. They need sports stadiums that can handle 100,000 people, as well as venues for fashion weeks, music performances, book festivals and countless trade fairs that can deal with sheer numbers. Design has a role to play in making such a stadium or an airport, or the concourse of a railway station, a dignified part of the city. It can turn what could otherwise be nothing more than a machine to process spectators in and out as quickly and as safely as possible into something that has a part to play in reinforcing the urbane qualities of city life.

The Albert Hall in London, which can seat 6,000 people as against an Olympic stadium of at least 80,000, might seem as modest in scale as a drawing room now. Yet its circular form and its stacked tiers create a space that is at once intimate and yet also designed to make the crowd aware of itself, to offer a sense of a shared experience. And that is precisely what the architects of Beijing's 2008 Olympic Stadium attempted to achieve in their design, planned in conjunction with the artist Ai Weiwei. 'We wanted to get away from the usual technocratic stadiums, with their architecture dominated by structural spans and digital screens,' Jacques Herzog commented. 'It is simple and almost archaically direct in its spatial impact. The architecture is the crowd, the proportions are intended to shift the spectators and the track and field events into the foreground.'

The way that a subway system or an airport system is designed can also reinforce or undermine the urban qualities of a city. Legible, handsome, easily negotiated public spaces make the individual feel part of something that they share with the rest of the city. Run-down, poorly maintained spaces reflect a lack of investment in the public realm, and so of confidence in the future of a city. They become somewhere to endure, not to experience. Some of us now live in cities in which we are always in the midst of crowds. The idea that the Tokyo metro employs people to push commuters closer together to fill every available inch on the trains to accommodate the crowds on the platform would once have seemed a particularly Japanese trauma. Now that level of overcrowding is commonplace in many cities. In the newer underground stations in London, where the platform is protected from the tracks by a glass screen pierced by sliding doors, tube users have acclimatized enough to the new reality to line up by the doors of incoming trains for a rush hour that can start at 6 a.m., as the construction workers and the cleaners head for work, and for off-peak fares that spread into the middle of the day.

We are inured to the understanding that our morning commute will involve being crammed together far beyond what any social norms would allow in other circumstances. And it is not just on transport systems that we must come to terms with the very close proximity of strangers. As pedestrians in the city, we negotiate pavements and platforms, concourses and crossings in which we can no longer move as individuals, but have to navigate and predict the movements of others.

We have to deal with the absence of presence exhibited by so many pedestrians now, a phenomenon that began with the advent of the headphones that characterized the personal stereo and the Walkman. Headphones allowed commuters and joggers to shut out the world around them. Portable suitcase-size ghetto blasters did something similar but with a wider impact, colonizing space as people moved.

The smartphone has taken this development to an extreme. Now it is not just a matter of listening to music, or taking a call in the middle of a face-to-face conversation. Concentrating on a personal screen in the midst of a crowd is an abdication of a shared individual responsibility as a pedestrian to interpret the nuances of human interaction with others to ensure that we do not collide on the pavement.

So the distinction between the permanent residents and the ever larger number of tourists is being eroded. Tourists use their screens to photograph each other or themselves with their digital devices on selfie sticks, while the locals are absorbed in the digital world through the portal of their smartphones.

When most of the world is characterized as urban, more than ever we must explore those characteristics of urbanism that offer us the chance to reinforce the essential qualities of a city. The city is humankind's most complex and extraordinary creation. It can be understood as a living organism. By their nature, living organisms can die when mistreated, or starved of resources, including people. At the same time, a city that is full of life is capable of endlessly adapting, flourishing in different circumstances, and with different inhabitants. Planned in the right way, it can support growing numbers of people.

A successful city is an entity that is continually reconfiguring itself, changing its social structure and meaning, even if its contours don't look very different. And when it does take on dramatic new forms, the measure of success is the degree to which it maintains its essence.

Acknowledgements

Much of this book was written in a farmhouse half an hour from Siena's Palazzo Pubblico. It was a chance to spend more time with Ambrogio Lorenzetti's famous mural, *The Allegory of Good and Bad Government*. For six centuries it has been both an inspiration and a caution, and not just to Siena's leaders. It is a reminder of how long we have tried to find ways to understand the nature of the city, simultaneously as a work of art, a moral and technical system and a reflection of how we live together.

Writing the book over the course of two summers was a comparatively quick process. Helen Conford, my clear-sighted editor at Penguin, helped shape the book into a set of questions about the nature of cities, and the book has further benefitted from the imaginative picture research of Cecilia Mackay and the careful copy-editing of Sarah Coward.

Questions about the nature of cities have fascinated me for many years. Looking at cities, how they change, and why they don't change, has fascinated me ever since I was growing up in the London of the 1950s and 60s, a city that from the prospect of 2016 seems both unimaginably different and eerily familiar.

It is twenty-five years since I wrote *The 100 Mile City*. That book began life as a commission to explore the impact of gentrification, but quickly morphed into an attempt to get to grips with the much more far-reaching set of changes that had reshaped so many cities, and made them part of a global system. As a journalist at the *Observer* and as editor of *Domus*, I was able to travel to see cities from Tokyo to Beijing, Jakarta to Melbourne, Johannesburg, Singapore, Seoul and Moscow.

It was *The 100 Mile City* that persuaded Ricky Burdett, director of the Cities Programme at the London School of Economics, to invite me to take part in 'The Urban Age', the series of conferences and studies undertaken over the course of a decade with the Alfred Herrhausen Society of Deutsche Bank. 'The Urban Age' was a uniquely privileged insight into the intricate and sometimes fraught connections between law, transport policy, development, politics and leadership, architecture and planning, sociology and ecology. 'The Urban Age' was a powerful argument for understanding the city as the product of all these issues, conventionally never considered as part of a coherent whole.

'The Urban Age' gave me the chance to begin work on some of the ideas that are crystallized here, and most importantly to learn from many thinkers in all those disciplines. In particular, I had the chance to learn from Richard Sennett and Saskia Sassen, Philipp Rode, Enrique Penalosa, Suketa Mehta, Jose Castillo Olca, Gerald Frug, Tony Travers, and many others.

I also had the opportunity to contribute to a record of those conferences in two substantial publications: *The Endless City*, and *Living in the Endless City*.

Without that experience and those dialogues, this would have been a very different book.

The experience has taught me that it is not enough only to observe, and report back. This is a book that tries to answer some questions about what makes a city, as well as to ask them.

Bibliography

Alexander, Christopher, *A City is Not a Tree.* 1965, reprinted 2015, Sustasis Press.

Alexander, Christopher, *A Pattern Language.* OUP, 1978.

Banham, Reyner, *Los Angeles: The Architecture of Four Ecologies.* Allen Lane, London, 1971.

Brook, Daniel, *A History of Future Cities.* Norton, New York, 2013.

Burdett, Richard and Sudjic, Deyan, *The Endless City.* Phaidon, London, 2008.

Burdett, Richard and Sudjic, Deyan (eds.), *Living in the Endless City.* Phaidon, London, 2011.

Caro, Robert, *The Power Broker: Robert Moses and the Fall of New York.* Knopf, New York, 1974.

Dickens, Charles, *Dombey and Son.* Penguin Books, London, 2002.

Ehrenhalt, Alan, *The Great Inversion.* Vintage, New York, 2013.

Engels, Friedrich, *The Condition of the Working Class in England*, Oxford World Classics Edition, 2009.

Gans, Herbert, *People and Plans.* Columbia University Press, New York, 1964.

Hall, Peter, *Great Planning Disasters*, revised edition. Penguin Books, London, 1981.

Jacobs, Jane, *The Death and Life of Great American Cities.* Random House, New York, 1961.

Jacobs, Jane, *The Economy of Cities.* Random House, New York, 1969.

Kirkland, Stephane, *Paris Reborn: Napoleon III, Baron Haussmann and the Quest to Build a Modern City.* St Martin's Press, New York, 2013.

Koolhaas, Rem, *Delirious New York.* Oxford University Press, 1978, new edition, Monacelli, New York, 1994.

McGuirk, Justin, *Radical Cities.* Verso, London, 2014.

Morris, William, *News From Nowhere.* Penguin Books, 1993.

Pamuk, Orhan, *The Museum of Innocence*, translated by Maureen

Freely. Faber, London, 2010.

Rossi, Aldo, *The Architecture of the City.* English translation MIT, Cambridge, 1984.

Rubinstein, Nicolai, *Political Ideas in Sienese Art: The Frescoes by Ambrogio Lorenzetti and Tadeo di Bartolo in the Palazzo Publico*, Journal of the Warburg and Courtauld Institutes. London July–Dec 1958.

Schickel, Richard, *The Disney Version*, revised edition. Pavilion, London 1986.

Sitte, Camillo, *Cities Built According to Artistic Principles*, 1889, translated 1945.

Sudjic, Deyan, *The Edifice Complex.* Allen Lane, London, 2006.

Sudjic, Deyan and Deutsch, Andre *The 100 Mile City*, London, 1992.

Venturi, Robert, Scott Brown, Denise and Izenour, Steven, *Learning from Las Vegas*, revised edition. Cambridge, MIT, 1977.

Whiteley, Nigel, *Reyner Banham: Historian of the Immediate Future.* MIT, 2002.

Zola, Émile, *Au Bonheur des Dames*, translated by Robin Buss. Penguin Books, London, 2001.

Picture Credits

Grateful acknowledgement is given to the following for permission to reproduce images:

p.iii – Rex Features; p.7 – Alamy; p.8 – Alamy; p.9 – Alamy; p.12 – Alamy; p.28 (top) - Getty Images; p.28 (bottom) – PA Images; p.37 – Alamy; p.38 – TopFoto; p.39 – Alamy; p.40 – Getty; p.41 - Getty; p.47 (top) - Fonds Prost. Académie d'architecture/Cité de l'architecture et du patrimoine/Archives d'architecture du XXe siècle; p.47 (bottom) – Wikimedia Commons; p.48 – private collection; p.49 - Evren Kalinbacak / Shutterstock; p.55 – TopFoto; p.56 – Wikimedia Commons; p.57 (top) – Rex Features; p.57 (bottom) – TopFoto; p.90 – Alamy; p.91– Rex Features; p.94 – Rex Features; p.95 – Getty; p.114 (top) – Getty; p.114 (bottom) – Alamy; p.115 (top) - Rex Features; p.115 (bottom) – Alamy; p.136 (top) - Buckminster Fuller and Shoji Sadao, *Dome Over Manhattan*, c.1960, Courtesy, The Estate of R. Buckminster Fuller; p.136 (bottom) – Alamy; p.138 - Eddie Hausner/NYT/Redux/Eyevine; p.139 – Getty Images; p.140 – private collection; p.141 – Getty; p.152 and 153 – © 2016 Photo Scala, Florence; p.165 – PA Images; p.178 – Art Institute of Chicago/The Art Archive; p.179 (top) - George Tooker, *The Subway*, 1950. Egg tempera on composition board, 18 1/8 × 36 1/8 in. (46 x 91.8cm). Whitney Museum of American Art, New York. © George Tooker. Photo: The Art Archive; p.179 (bottom) – Alamy; p.180 – Museum of London/Getty Images; p.189 – © Hiroji Kubota/Magnum Photos; p.190 – © Martin Roemers/Panos Pictures; p.191 – Alamy; p.200 (top) – TopFoto; p.200 (bottom) – Facebook/Frank Gehry; p.201 (top) – © Apple Inc/Foster + Partners; p.201 (bottom) – Google/Heatherwick Studio/Bjarke Ingels Group; p.210 – Alamy; p.211 – EPA/Camera Press, London; p.212 - © Alamy; p.213 – Alamy.

Index

Index

Index